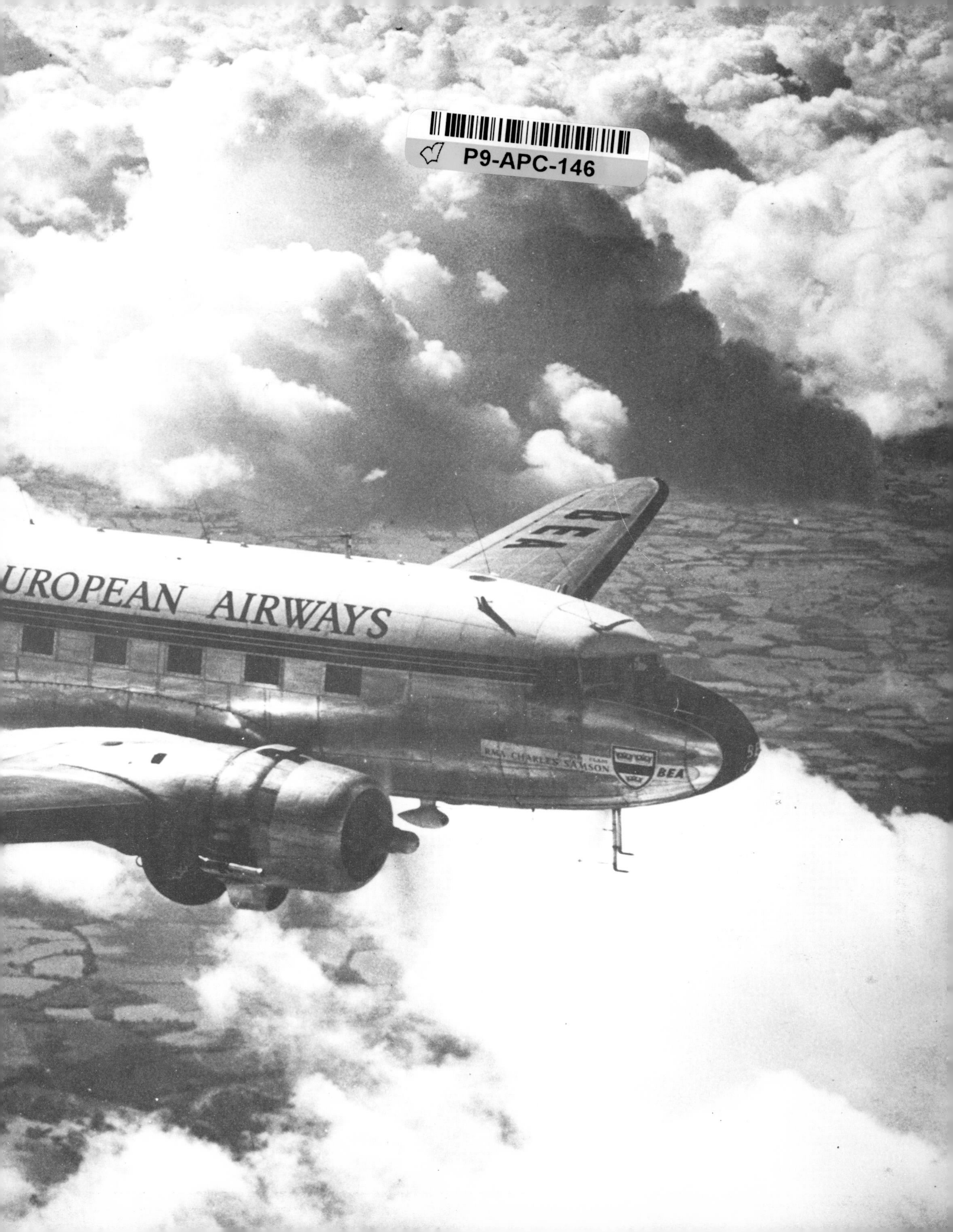
BEA
UROPEAN AIRWAYS
RMA CHARLES SAMSON
BEA

DOUGLAS DC~3 DAKOTA

M.J. Hooks

Foulis

Haynes

ISBN 0 85429 449 X

A FOULIS Aircraft Book

First published 1985

Published by:
Haynes Publishing Group
Sparkford,
Yeovil,
Somerset BA22 7JJ

Distributed in USA by:
Haynes Publications Inc.
861 Lawrence Drive,
Newbury Park,
California 91320, USA

Produced by:
**Winchmore Publishing
Services Limited,**
40 Triton Square,
London NW1 3HG

Printed in England

Further titles in this series will be published at
regular intervals. For information on new titles
please contact your bookseller or write to the
publisher.

Contents

Genesis

In the period following World War I air transport was a hotch-potch of surplus military aircraft flown by surplus military pilots. The urge to fly came in the wake of a costly war, mostly from pilots who had been trained at government expense and had little other qualification to help them return to civilian life.

The general public were understandably wary of aircraft; after all, their primary purpose had been first to train pilots and then to enable these men to kill the enemy.

Since most wartime aircraft were not expected to last very long and were built under conditions which required rapid production, it was not surprising that there were many accidents in the early post-war days involving surplus military aircraft pressed into use for joy-riding or barnstorming. But there were men with the foresight to realise the potential of air travel, such as Roe, de Havilland, Handley Page, Dornier, Junkers and Farman in Europe; while in the United States there were Northrop, Boeing, Martin and Douglas. These men were all to become major manufacturers, but without the push from those who had taken the initiative and formed airlines, like Jack Frye, Cyrus Smith and Eddie Rickenbacker, the present-day air transport system would have taken much longer to evolve.

Aircraft were being built for the specialised business of passenger carrying on both sides of the Atlantic; the early ones betrayed their military ancestry and were biplanes in most cases. In Holland, Fokker began a long line of wooden high-wing monoplanes, moving up from single to twin then to triple engine installations as the aircraft grew larger, while in Germany Junkers began an even longer line of metal transports whose corrugated skinning became a trademark, earning a reputation for strength and

reliability. In England, the sheer size of the Handley Page H.P.42 four-engine biplane airliner was impressive, but it was also accused of having a built-in headwind.

In the USA, the twin-engine Curtiss Condor of 1933 was the last of the biplane airliners; even as deliveries began the new designs of fast, low-wing monoplanes were on the drawing boards and Boeing's twin-engine Model 247, an all-metal monoplane with a retractable undercarriage, was revolutionising air transport with its 200 mph (322 km/h) cruising speed (a 50 mph [80 km/h] increase on the other types of airliner in service), accommodation for ten passengers and up to 400 lb (181 kg) of mail and a range, in the Model 247D, of 745 miles (1,199 km).

Donald Douglas, who had built a number of single-engine biplanes

Top: The beginning of a long line; the DC-1 X223 with a TWA badge.

Above: Swiss Air Lines' DC-2s HB-ITA and -ITO share the Zurich/Dubendorf tarmac in the mid-1930s with one of two Clark GA-43s also operated by the airline.

including the World Cruisers used by the US Army in its first round-the-world flight in 1924, was asked by Jack Frye, President of TWA, to quote on a specification for an all-metal, three-engine monoplane with a capacity for 12 passengers, a crew of two, payload of 2,300 lb (1,043 kg) with full fuel tanks and a maximum gross weight of 14,200 lb (6,441 kg). A range of 1,080 miles (1,738 km), minimum sea-level top speed of 185 mph (298 km/h) and cruising speed of 146 mph (235 km/h), landing speed of 65 mph (105 km/h) and ceiling of

Above: The second DC-2 sale by Fokker was A-500 for Austrian President Dollfuss delivered in September 1934. It passed to Swissair in April 1936 as HB-ISA and was re-sold the same year to LAPE as EC-AAA.

Below: Close-up of a CLS DC-2; note the functional but ugly landing lights in the nose. In the DC-3 these were moved to the outer wing leading edges.

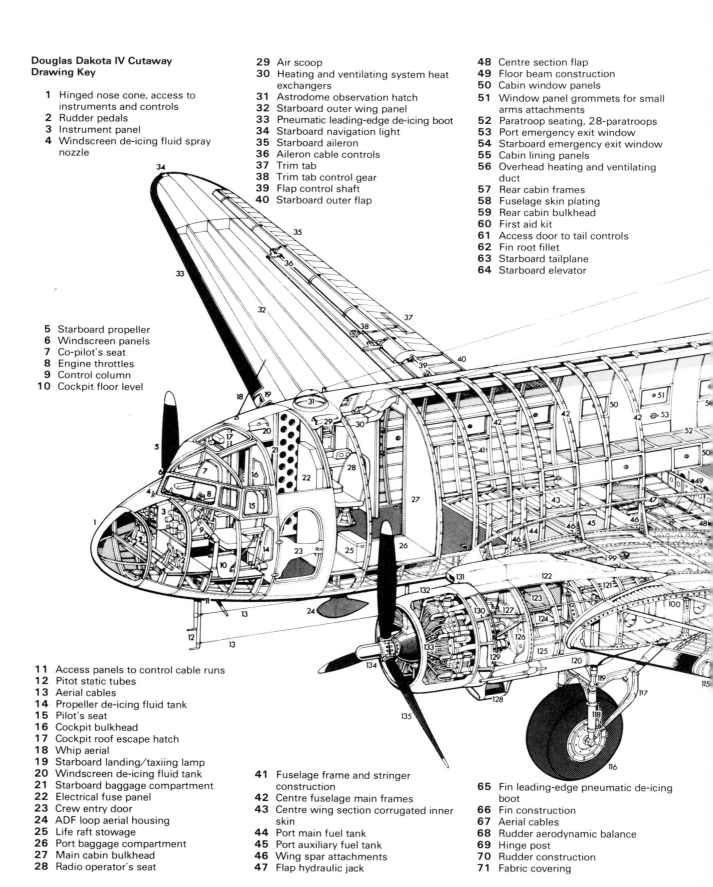

Douglas Dakota IV Cutaway Drawing Key

1 Hinged nose cone, access to instruments and controls
2 Rudder pedals
3 Instrument panel
4 Windscreen de-icing fluid spray nozzle

5 Starboard propeller
6 Windscreen panels
7 Co-pilot's seat
8 Engine throttles
9 Control column
10 Cockpit floor level

11 Access panels to control cable runs
12 Pitot static tubes
13 Aerial cables
14 Propeller de-icing fluid tank
15 Pilot's seat
16 Cockpit bulkhead
17 Cockpit roof escape hatch
18 Whip aerial
19 Starboard landing/taxiing lamp
20 Windscreen de-icing fluid tank
21 Starboard baggage compartment
22 Electrical fuse panel
23 Crew entry door
24 ADF loop aerial housing
25 Life raft stowage
26 Port baggage compartment
27 Main cabin bulkhead
28 Radio operator's seat

29 Air scoop
30 Heating and ventilating system heat exchangers
31 Astrodome observation hatch
32 Starboard outer wing panel
33 Pneumatic leading-edge de-icing boot
34 Starboard navigation light
35 Starboard aileron
36 Aileron cable controls
37 Trim tab
38 Trim tab control gear
39 Flap control shaft
40 Starboard outer flap

41 Fuselage frame and stringer construction
42 Centre fuselage main frames
43 Centre wing section corrugated inner skin
44 Port main fuel tank
45 Port auxiliary fuel tank
46 Wing spar attachments
47 Flap hydraulic jack

48 Centre section flap
49 Floor beam construction
50 Cabin window panels
51 Window panel grommets for small arms attachments
52 Paratroop seating, 28-paratroops
53 Port emergency exit window
54 Starboard emergency exit window
55 Cabin lining panels
56 Overhead heating and ventilating duct
57 Rear cabin frames
58 Fuselage skin plating
59 Rear cabin bulkhead
60 First aid kit
61 Access door to tail controls
62 Fin root fillet
63 Starboard tailplane
64 Starboard elevator

65 Fin leading-edge pneumatic de-icing boot
66 Fin construction
67 Aerial cables
68 Rudder aerodynamic balance
69 Hinge post
70 Rudder construction
71 Fabric covering

6

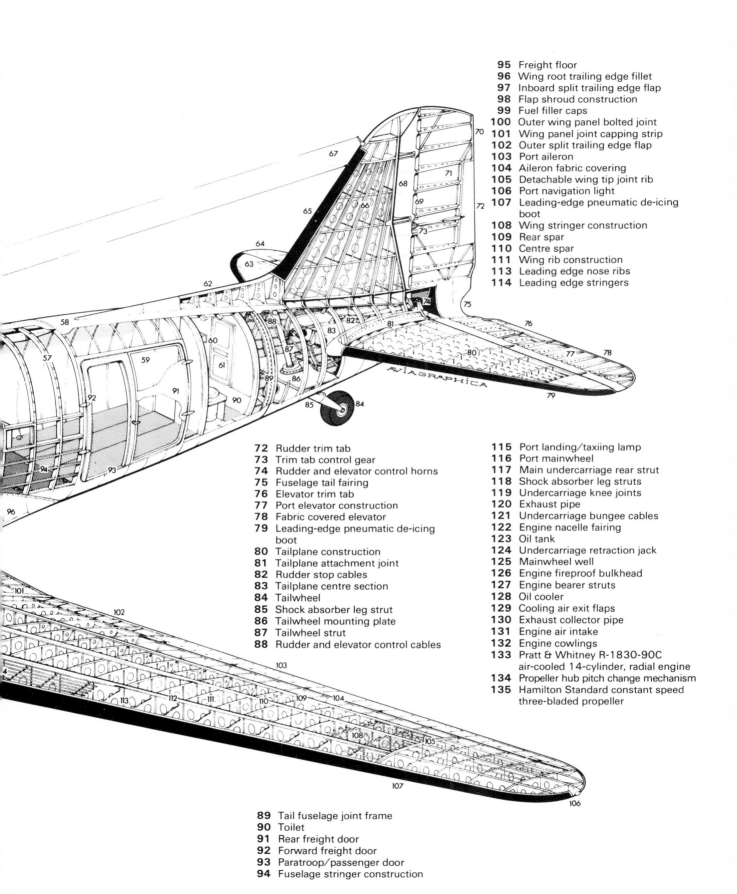

95 Freight floor
96 Wing root trailing edge fillet
97 Inboard split trailing edge flap
98 Flap shroud construction
99 Fuel filler caps
100 Outer wing panel bolted joint
101 Wing panel joint capping strip
102 Outer split trailing edge flap
103 Port aileron
104 Aileron fabric covering
105 Detachable wing tip joint rib
106 Port navigation light
107 Leading-edge pneumatic de-icing boot
108 Wing stringer construction
109 Rear spar
110 Centre spar
111 Wing rib construction
113 Leading edge nose ribs
114 Leading edge stringers

72 Rudder trim tab
73 Trim tab control gear
74 Rudder and elevator control horns
75 Fuselage tail fairing
76 Elevator trim tab
77 Port elevator construction
78 Fabric covered elevator
79 Leading-edge pneumatic de-icing boot
80 Tailplane construction
81 Tailplane attachment joint
82 Rudder stop cables
83 Tailplane centre section
84 Tailwheel
85 Shock absorber leg strut
86 Tailwheel mounting plate
87 Tailwheel strut
88 Rudder and elevator control cables

115 Port landing/taxiing lamp
116 Port mainwheel
117 Main undercarriage rear strut
118 Shock absorber leg struts
119 Undercarriage knee joints
120 Exhaust pipe
121 Undercarriage bungee cables
122 Engine nacelle fairing
123 Oil tank
124 Undercarriage retraction jack
125 Mainwheel well
126 Engine fireproof bulkhead
127 Engine bearer struts
128 Oil cooler
129 Cooling air exit flaps
130 Exhaust collector pipe
131 Engine air intake
132 Engine cowlings
133 Pratt & Whitney R-1830-90C air-cooled 14-cylinder, radial engine
134 Propeller hub pitch change mechanism
135 Hamilton Standard constant speed three-bladed propeller

89 Tail fuselage joint frame
90 Toilet
91 Rear freight door
92 Forward freight door
93 Paratroop/passenger door
94 Fuselage stringer construction

OK-AIH was the first of four DC-3s bought by CLS from Fokker in August 1937, the others following in January 1938 (2) and January 1939. All were taken over by Lufthansa on the occupation of Czechoslovakia.

21,000 ft (6,400 m) were required – a daunting specification for 1932.

The knowledge that Pratt & Whitney and Wright had new engines under construction which would give considerably more power than the engines then available decided Douglas to go for a twin-engine design. He knew that he had to beat the Boeing 247's performance, and chose for the wing a modified version of the airfoil used on the recent Northrop Alpha – Northrop was a subsidiary of Douglas at that time. As the new design progressed a title had to be found and it became the DC-1 – Douglas Commercial Model No. 1.

In June 1933, the DC-1, registered X-223Y, was rolled out, having cost in excess of $300,000 to build – Douglas had quoted a price to TWA of $125,000. The first flight on 1 July was eventful and there were problems with the engines which kept cutting out in the climb, only to come back to life in the descent. This was later found to be a fault in the carburettors and was easily cured.

An extensive flight test programme was undertaken during which it was discovered that the DC-1 could be landed safely with the undercarriage retracted, since the wheels protruded below the engine nacelles. This discovery was made quite by accident during some take-offs and landings, when apparently each of the crew members thought the other was operating the pump to lower the undercarriage, but neither did! The only damage was to the propellers. There is a story that a pilot subsequently made a dead-stick wheels-up landing in a Dakota when both engines stopped, but in this case he brought the propeller blades round by using the starter motor so that each side had a vertical blade and managed to land without even damaging the propellers.

Testing continued, and during the speed trials the DC-1 reached 227 mph (365 km/h), a performance being achieved by contemporary racing aircraft. The Douglas engineers devised a formula for measuring an engine's power output in flight and were able to produce tables which enabled pilots to work out their most efficient cruise power and altitude. Using these formulae increased the efficiency and economics by some 20 per cent according to Douglas, which made the DC-1 not only the fastest transport but also the most economical; Douglas had achieved his target of beating the Boeing 247, good though that aeroplane was.

The DC-1 was also quiet when it was furnished, with an interior sound level of only 72 decibels at 200 mph (322 km/h); considerable thought had gone into this aspect and the cabin furnishings were designed to absorb noise.

Jack Frye of TWA could hardly fail to be impressed by the

LOT (Polish Air Lines) chose Bristol Pegasus VI engines for its two DC-2Bs SP-ASK and -ASL, handed over in July and August 1935.

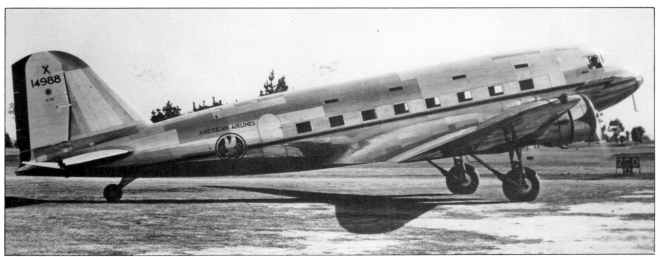

performance, economics and comfort, and placed an order for 20 (later increased to 28), but by this time a successor, the DC-2, was well under way and only one DC-1 was built.

In December 1933 the DC-1 was officially handed over to TWA at Los Angeles and operated on a number of routes, later carrying out a number of record-setting flights before being sold to Howard Hughes. It passed into British ownership as G-AFIF in 1938, then to French, and eventually was used by the Spanish Republican Government to evacuate their officials from Spain when the Nationalists came to power. In December 1940, the DC-1's luck ran out at Malaga when an engine failed on take-off and it crash-landed on the runway without injuries to the passengers or crew. It was a complete write-off – a sad end for an historic aircraft.

Meanwhile, TWA's DC-2s were taking shape on the production line, and the airline received its first aircraft, NC 13711, on 14 May 1934; it entered service four days later.

The DC-2 was basically a stretch of the DC-1; the fuselage was two feet longer which increased the passenger capacity from 12 to 14 in two rows of 40-in (102-cm) wide lounge seats divided by a 16-in (41-cm) aisle – positively luxurious compared with most present-day high-density jetliners!

There was a separate window for each seat, and the 710-hp Wright Cyclone supercharged engines were claimed to give a maximum speed of 225 mph (362 km/h) at 18,000 feet (5,486 m); the landing speed was a mere 58 mph (93 km/h).

As the new fleet built up, so TWA revenue and market share soared. The airline paid $65,000 per aircraft which meant a loss of $266,000 to Douglas for the total TWA order but other orders soon began to come in to take the company back into the black.

The speed of the DC-2 made coast-to-coast schedules a practicality, and the TWA overnight New York to Los Angeles flight took less than 18 hours, perhaps a long time by

today's standards but 50 years ago a very great step in airline progress.

The designation allotted to the early aircraft was DC-2-112, and following delivery of the first 20 production models to TWA, General Air Lines received four DC-2-112s, Eastern eight, TWA another eight and then the designation changed. Pan Am took delivery of six DC-2-118As and Bs and American Airlines ten DC-2-120s.

With the main American carriers operating the new airliner, interest had been aroused in Europe,

Above: The first DST-114 as originally registered X14988; it subsequently became NC14988. Note absence of fin fillet as compared with production models.

Below: An elegant 1940 DC-3 interior configured as a 21-seater.

particularly in The Netherlands. Anthony Fokker had visited the Douglas factory at Santa Monica in 1933 to see the DC-1 and had been so impressed that he ordered a DC-2.

Fokker's steel tube, wood and fabric airliners had served several European airlines well, but the advent of the DC-2 spelled the end of the road for them; Fokker, quick to realise this, purchased the manufacturing and European sales rights of the DC-2 for $100,000 and was eventually to sell 39 DC-2s, but no Douglas aircraft were built in The Netherlands.

In 1934, the British company Airspeed acquired the licence to manufacture 15 types of Fokker aircraft, together with manufacturing and sales rights of the DC-2 in the UK, Eire and the Channel Islands but expansion of military orders received by Airspeed killed the project.

Fokker supplied DC-2s to KLM,

Deutsche Lufthansa, Avio Linee Italiana, the Austrian Government, Swissair, LAPE (Spain), the French Government, LOT (Poland) and Czechoslovakian Air Lines.

Like the TWA DC-2s, the KLM aircraft began their operations with plenty of press coverage, and the 15-year-old airline introduced its new DC-2 on the 9,000-mile (14,484-km) schedule from Amsterdam to Batavia. A few weeks later, in October 1934, KLM's first aircraft, PH-AJU, christened Uiver (Stork), was entered for the prestigious England to Australia Air Race. Competing against 20 entrants from six countries, some of which, like the de Havilland Comets, were specially designed for such flights, the DC-2, under the command of KLM pilots Parmentier and Moll, came second in both the speed and handicap sections behind Scott and Campbell Black in a Comet.

The success of this flight could

not fail to impress other airlines, and within a year of the prototype's first flight more than 100 DC-2s were in service in 12 countries on both sides of the Atlantic. A survey carried out by Douglas revealed that DC-2s had by that time topped 20 million miles (32 million km) in service and were flying about 75,000 miles (120,698 km) every 24 hours. During 15 million miles (24 million km) of flying in North and South America in this period the aircraft recorded 98.8 per cent efficiency, an astonishing figure for the mid-1930s, particularly since it was achieved with brand new aircraft designed to a new concept. Technology was indeed beginning to make itself felt.

Impressed by the airlines' performances with the DC-2, the US Navy bought one designated

A patriotic slogan above the C-47A production line at Long Beach – from the front the six visible aircraft are 43-15217 to -212 (line numbers 3070 to -65).

DC-2-125, taking delivery in December 1934. The Navy designation was R2D-1, and the US Marine Corps took delivery shortly afterwards of another R2D-1. In all, the Navy had three aircraft and the Marines two; they served for some years before being destroyed in accidents or withdrawn from use but the third Navy aircraft was sold to North American Aviation in the early 1950s and saw considerable civilian service.

The US Army Air Corps bought a single DC-2-153 for evaluation in 1935 as an XC-32 and were obviously impressed; two more were bought, a DC-2-173 and a -346. Both were VIP transports and were designated YC-34. All three aircraft dropped their X and Y prefixes after entering service. The Army then placed an order for 18 aircraft, DC-2-145s, which became C-33s; they had larger tails than the earlier models and a cargo-loading door, a feature which was to make the C-47 series such valuable transports.

USAAC deliveries were phased over nine months, being completed in January 1937; like the civil models they were powered by 750-hp Wright R-1820-25 Cyclone engines. In a natural progression, the Army ordered 35 of a newer model, the C-39 (DC-2-243) with R-1820-35 Cyclones of 975 hp. This used a DC-3 type centre section, tail and undercarriage and stemmed from the experimental C-38 which had been converted from a C-33 to incorporate a DC-3 tail; the C-39s were 16-seaters.

Before leaving the military DC-2 variants, mention must be made of the C-41 (1,200 hp R-1820-21 Twin Wasp engines) and the C-42 with similarly powered R-1820-53 Cyclones; both were conversions on the line from C-39s, and two more C-42s were subsequently converted. A C-39 was in fact the last aircraft to leave the DC-2 production line. The military aircraft undertook considerable transport work and were supplemented in 1942 by the impressment of 24 commercial models from US domestic operators. They received the designation C-32A and had 740-hp Cyclone engines but no cargo door.

The British Purchasing Commission bought an initial batch of 12 DC-2s from US airlines in 1941, and these were followed by another 13 but of this batch only 10 were delivered. They supplemented the RAF's meagre force of transports in Asia, serving with Nos 31 and 117 Squadrons; nine came from American Airlines, five each from TWA and Delta, and three from Pan American. The RAF DC-2s saw service in Iraq alongside ancient Vickers Valentia biplane transports, helping to quell a rebellion in Egypt where, among other operations, they made two flights to Stalingrad, and in India and Burma carrying supplies in one direction and casualties in the other. Inevitably, a number were lost due to crashes and enemy action, and several served with the Indian Airline Tata. One of these, an ex-American Airlines aircraft, was struck off charge by Tata in June 1945, the latest date recorded for any of the RAF DC-2s.

Another DC-2 to see military service was a former KLM and AB Aerotransport aircraft which had been bought by Count von Rosen and made available to the Finnish Air Force in January 1940 for the war against the Soviet Union. Fitted with bomb racks under the centre section for 24 26-lb (12-kg) bombs and a dorsal turret with a 7.7-mm machine gun, it is known to have operated against a Russian airfield. It was later joined by two other DC-2s which the Germans had captured; one of the aircraft was subsequently re-engined with 1,000-hp Russian M-62 engines.

LOT Polish Airlines had been responsible for an earlier change of engines when they ordered two DC-2s in 1935 with the stipulation that they be powered by 750-hp Bristol Pegasus VI engines – these were widely used in Poland and were being licence-built by Skoda.

The development of the Pegasus-powered DC-2 was shared between Douglas and Bristol. A plan to fit Renault-built nine-cylinder engines to a DC-2 did not materialise although one aircraft was bought through Fokker for tests.

Total production of the DC-2 reached 193, of which 78 were delivered to US civil customers, 62 to the US military, 40 to Fokker for onward sale to European customers and 13 to other overseas customers. Additional to these were five sent unassembled to Japan following delivery of a complete example, J-BBOI, in 1934 to Dai Nippon Airways, and two DC-2-120s delivered to American Airlines as parts in 1935.

The success of the DC-2 encouraged Douglas to consider stretching it to provide sleeping bunks, a feature which was offered on the Curtiss Condor biplane which had a wider fuselage than the DC-2.

Sleeper services had begun with the Condor in May 1934 between Los Angeles and Dallas, but the biplane was nowhere near as fast as the Douglas aircraft, so a sleeper version of the latter could soon be expected to scoop up the market.

C.R. Smith of American Airlines, operating 15 DC-2s, was enthusiastic about a sleeper version but for some reason Douglas was not. However, he was persuaded to carry out a design study when Smith offered to place an order for 20 aircraft. The DC-3 legend had begun.

The project was christened DST for Douglas Sleeper Transport; it had a wider and longer fuselage with room for 14 bunk beds, longer wing and a larger fin and rudder than the DC-2. Initial wind tunnel tests showed a stability problem resulting from a change in the centre of gravity, but this was eventually cured as interior designers got to work on the mock-up. They studied the effects of colours on passengers,

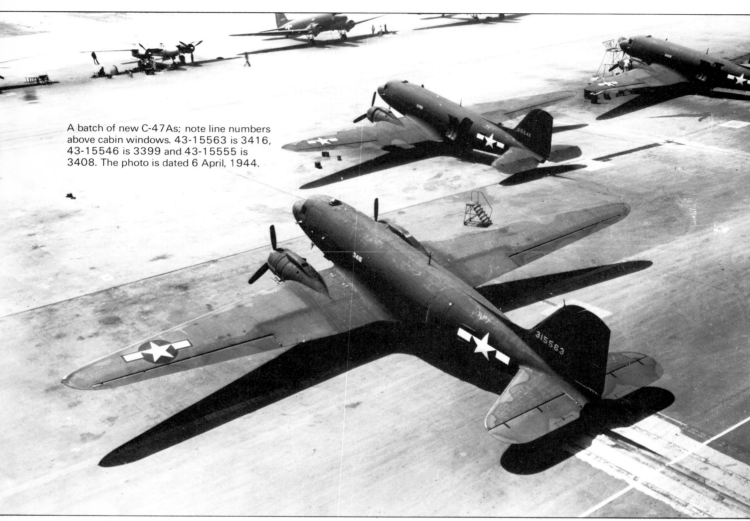

A batch of new C-47As; note line numbers above cabin windows. 43-15563 is 3416, 43-15546 is 3399 and 43-15555 is 3408. The photo is dated 6 April, 1944.

particularly with regard to air sickness, and came up with a restful scheme of subdued colours.

New cockpit and instrument panel lighting was introduced and a new hydraulic undercarriage design did away with the need to pump the gear up or down. Foot brakes were another innovation.

On 17 December 1935, the DST was rolled out and made its first flight. Unlike the memorable first flight of the DC-2, this one was uneventful. The engines in the prototype were 850-hp Wright Cyclone GR-1820-G2s but production aircraft were available with five different models of Cyclone.

Since the DST was designed with luxury accommodation it is worth describing the cabin. It was 19 ft 5½ in (5.9 m) long, 7 ft 8 in

(2.3 m) wide and 6 ft 4½ in (1.9 m) high, and was divided into four sections with a centre aisle. Each contained two 36-in (91-cm) wide facing seats which could be folded together to form the lower berth, while the 30-in (76-cm) wide upper berth was pulled down from the ceiling. DSTs could be distinguished externally from DC-3s by the four small slit 'eyebrow' windows in each side of the fuselage above the normal cabin windows – they were provided for occupants of the upper berths. A reading lamp, stewardess call button and clothes net were provided for each berth and another innovation was the separate dressing rooms for men and women, with mirrors, towels and running water and separate toilet facilities for each room. A

galley providing hot meals was at the front of the main cabin and baggage compartment at the rear. Later aircraft had an enclosed stateroom with two berths or four seats which could be booked at an enhanced fare. Brochure figures given at the launch of the DST gave its maximum speed as 212 mph (341 km/h), cruising at 180 mph (290 km/h), landing speed 64 mph (103 km/h) and service ceiling 20,800 ft (6,340 m), although its absolute ceiling was 23,100 feet (7,041 m).

A big plus point was the operating cost which was given in the company's 1935 annual report as 69 cents a mile, about the same as the Ford Trimotor but with twice the capacity on a ton/mile basis. Between New York and Chicago non-stop, the DST operating cost was around $800, again about the same as the Trimotor but the latter stopped at Pittsburgh and Cleveland since it had to trade range for payload. Flying non-stop, the DST could almost triple the Ford's payload.

The best news in the report was that the company was developing a 21-passenger luxury version of the DST for the airlines, but meantime American Airlines inaugurated its DST sleeper service on 8 June 1936 between Los Angeles and Chicago. Coast-to-coast service followed in September, linking New York with Los Angeles.

American DSTs were rolling rapidly off the production lines and the airline had taken delivery of its first batch of eight, including the prototype, within 14 weeks of receiving the first. The order was subsequently increased to 15 aircraft by deliveries of one aircraft in March 1938, four between October 1939 and June 1940, and the final two in August 1940.

United Air Lines was to prove the biggest user of the DST; the first six of its order for eight were handed over in July 1937 with the next two the following month and the remainder, like American's, were spread over a period. United was the first airline to lose a DST when the fourth aircraft to be delivered, NC 18108, was written off in a forced landing following an engine fire at Cleveland, Ohio, on 24 May 1938. The last United

DST, delivered in June 1941, was also the last built.

Other customers were Western Air Express (two delivered in June and July 1937) and Eastern who had five. Total DST production was therefore 40, of which 21 were DSTs, with Wright-Cyclone engines, and 19 DST-As, with Pratt & Whitney Twin Wasps. The Cyclones were supplied in a number of sub-variants ranging from 850 to 1,000 hp, while the Twin Wasps were 900 hp; the DST-A was developed specifically for United but Western also chose this variant.

In 1942, the 37 surviving DSTs were impressed into USAAF service under four designations; 15 were C-48Bs (13 from United and two from Western), two C-48Cs (both United), 15 C-49Es (all American) and five C-49Fs (four from Eastern and one from United). Mention has been made of the Eastern DST crash; United's NC 18146 narrowly missed impressment by flying into a mountain near Salt Lake City on 2 May 1942, and Eastern lost one when it flew into trees at Atlanta on 26 February 1941, during an instrument let-down. Surprisingly, 28 of the DSTs survived the war to be civilianised again, some of them lasting into the 1970s.

From the foregoing it might appear that the DST and DC-3 were developed separately, but this was not so. The early promise of

the DST design was such that Douglas developed the DC-3 in parallel and the production line was a mixed one, the first true DC-3 being delivered to American Airlines on 18 August 1936, hard on the heels of that company's seventh DST a month previously. By November 1936, American had received 11 DC-3s and the next aircraft off the line was shipped to France at the end of that month for onward delivery to Russia – probably the inspiration for the many licence-built versions that were to emerge from Russian factories as the PS-84, later known as the Lisunov Li-2. These early DC-3s had 850-hp Wright Cyclone engines, but in later versions the power increased to 900 hp, and by 1939, to 1,000 hp.

Fokker received the next DC-3 for KLM; this was later to be leased to BOAC and was shot down over the Bay of Biscay on 1 June 1943.

Production was now well under way, and United Air Lines with its Boeing 247s was feeling the pinch with early competition from TWA and American Airlines DC-2s. At the time of its introduction, the 247 was certainly a revolutionary design but the advent of the DC-2 marked the beginning of the end for the smaller Boeing airliner.

United was left with no alternative but to order the DC-3; however, since the competition was using the same type and since United's routes required crossing the Rockies, the airline decided to order DC-3s with the newer 900-hp Pratt & Whitney Hornet engines. Although they cost more, an increase of 14 mph (22.5 km/h) in cruising speed and a higher ceiling of 23,400 ft (7,132 m) were compensatory factors and the first was delivered to United on 23 December 1936.

By December 1937, two years after the first DST had flown, Douglas was turning out DC-3s at the rate of 36 a month and had a

The sole XC-32 was similar to the DC-2, differing only in equipment details.

backlog of orders valued at more than $7.25 million, of which $5.25 million were for foreign customers.

The airliner was having a profound effect on operating costs and airline profits. While the DC-2 had been the first airliner to make a reasonable return on investment, the DC-3 was able to improve considerably on its predecessor. The seat mile cost went down from 4.8 to 3.4 cents and maintenance costs, always a source of concern to the airlines, went down as a result of the DC-3's design which simplified replacement of both major and minor parts. For instance, the new engine mounts had permanent fittings for fuel and electrical connections enabling an engine change to be made in two hours, and wing panels could be easily replaced.

It was small wonder that both large and small US airlines were eager to replace their motley collection of aircraft of all sizes from the Ford, Fokker and Stinson trimotors to the Curtiss Condor biplanes and orders poured in to Douglas.

By the beginning of 1937 US airlines were carrying an average of 3,400 passengers, 10 tons (10.16 tonnes) of express and 23 tons (23.37 tonnes) of mail every 24 hours. There were more than 60,000 miles (96,558 km) of air routes operated by US-registered aircraft on scheduled services, and of these 28,000 miles (45,060 km) were in the US with

the balance outside. Domestic airlines flew about 196,000 miles (315,423 km) daily and a map of scheduled airline operations within the US at 1 January 1937, showed 74 routes operated by 25 airlines; a large percentage of the aircraft used were DC-3s.

American Airlines secured an exclusive contract in 1936 with the Deutsche Zeppelin-Reederei to fly their transatlantic passengers on from the airship station at Lakehurst to New York and vice versa, the first such flight taking place on 9 May with passengers from the airship *Hindenburg*.

Development of the new airliners went hand-in-hand with development of airports and navigation aids; by January 1937 there were 2,342 airports and landing fields in the US, of which 705 were partially or fully lighted for night use. The total included 738 municipal and 451 commercial airports, the balance being made up of intermediate and auxiliary landing fields, military fields and private, government and State airports and landing fields. An airways traffic control system had become necessary, and the first units were established at Newark, Chicago and Cleveland. There were 22,245 miles (35,799 km) of lighted airways indicating routes compared to 15,000 (24,140 km) in 1930, and 500 meteorological stations were in use along the airways.

For three years the DC-3 virtually cornered the market as a fast, twin-

engine transport, but the war clouds were gathering in Europe, threatening to cut off the civil requirements which Fokker had been meeting as the Douglas agent; by the outbreak of war the Dutch company had sold 62 DC-3s and -3As.

The DC-3 customers were KLM (24), Russia (18), Swissair (five), CLS, Czechoslovakia (four), ABA, Sweden (four), Sabena (two), LARES, Romania (two), and one each to Air France, Aer Lingus and China. While the war curtailed European sales, the demand for the home market continued until the US entered the war, at which time DSTs and DC-3s for civil airlines were not delivered but were converted on the production line to military standards and eventually delivered to the USAAF. The DC-3 had gone to war. The USAAF, already using a number of DC-2s, was more than interested in the DC-3.

Below: American Airlines' DC-2-120 NC14278 served with them from December 1934 until bought by the British Purchasing Commission in May 1941. On delivery to No. 267 RAF Squadron as HK867, it crashed at Freetown, Sierra Leone, in September 1942 following a collision with Hurricane Z4257 but survived to serve with the USAAF as a C-32A serialled 42-53530.

Below left: A pre-war scene at Amsterdam/Schiphol with a KLM DC-3 (foreground) and DC-2.

C-47 and Variants in Service

Whether the State Department's budget would have allowed large military purchases in peacetime is debatable, but the inevitability of war acted as a spur and the Air Force submitted its requirements for changes in the aircraft to Douglas.

The necessity for carrying heavier loads than civil transports made a strengthened cabin floor and rear fuselage mandatory; large double loading doors in the left side of the fuselage behind the wing were needed to permit Jeeps and other vehicles to be loaded and external racks for supply packs had to be fitted. These requirements obviously dictated more powerful engines, and the 1,200-hp Pratt & Whitney R-1830-92 was chosen for the first batch of aircraft. This enabled the maximum operating weight to be increased from 25,000 lb (11,340 kg) to 29,300 lb (13,290 kg) initially; subsequently it was to go up to 35,000 lb (15,876 kg). The smart airline interior was replaced by utility bucket seats facing inwards along the cabin walls.

When the USAAF placed orders in September 1940 for the C-47 as it was to be designated, it was necessary to open a production line at a new factory in Long Beach, California, as the main Douglas plant at Santa Monica was fully committed to production of other types. The first contract covered 147 aircraft and this was followed a year later by another, this time for 1,900. Orders of such volume necessitated another factory and one was opened at Oklahoma City. New production techniques had to be learned quickly to enable the vastly increased tempo of production to

be achieved.

The first C-47-DL (the suffix indicating Douglas Long Beach) was delivered to the USAAF on 23 December 1941 and was followed by another 964 from the same factory.

Improvements in cabin heating and upgrading of the electrical system from 12 to 24 volts led to the next series, the C-47A-DL and -DK, the latter built in Oklahoma City. These two variants totalled 5,253 production models and accounted for more than 50 per cent of the total aircraft eventually acquired by the USAAF. The name Skytrain was adopted for the C-47 series.

The C-47B-DL and -DK were intended for high-altitude operations and had 1,200-hp R-1830-90C engines fitted with two-stage blowers and further improved heating. Production of these models totalled 3,232 and in fact ran right through to the last production C-47, handed over to the USAAF on 23 October 1945. Although built as C-47Bs, the great majority were converted to C-47Ds by the simple process of

Above: This batch of C-47Bs for Russia show the red star on a white disc, a marking which seems to be peculiar to early lease-lend aircraft from USA.

Top: C-47B 44-76890, a brand-new lease-lend aircraft for Russia, photographed from the cockpit of an RAF Dakota.

removing the engine blowers when it was found that the R-1830-90Cs were not performing satisfactorily with the blowers.

A batch of 133 navigational trainers was built at Oklahoma City as TC-47B-DKs; the next designation to be allocated was XC-47C-DL for an aircraft fitted with Edo amphibious floats. Each float could carry 300 US gallons of fuel which obviously reduced the payload considerably. Historians seem unable to agree on whether or not production was undertaken but there was also one YC-47C; one source quotes Edo as receiving an order for 150 sets of floats but it is thought that only two others were converted, by the USAAF. What is certain is that there was only one XCG-17, a C-47-DL with its engines removed for trials as a transport glider in 1944. Tests had been undertaken with a C-47, cutting its engines at 5,000 ft (1,524 m) and coming down to a deadstick landing to prove that the aircraft had a reasonable gliding capability. It had, and the next step was to tow a standard C-47 with another, using the engines of both for take-off and cutting the engines of the towed aircraft to glide back to a landing. With both propellers feathered, the C-47 had a glide ratio of 14 to 1, shallower than the purpose-designed Wacos then in use, and with a stalling speed of only 35 mph (56 km/h) compared with the Waco CG-4's 55 mph (88 km/h). Tow speeds of up to 290 mph (467 km/h) (but not by a C-47!) could be achieved against a conventional glider's 200 mph (322 km/h) limit.

The changes made on the XCG-17 included replacement of the engine by hemispherical streamlined cones, removal of unnecessary and weighty interior equipment, including the forward baggage compartments and installation of a new floor to enable cargo to be loaded further forward, compensating for the lack of engine weight. The tests, carried out at Clinton Army Base, Ohio, were completely successful but by the time they had ended the USAAF's requirement for combat gliders had gone and no further development took place. However, news of the towing experiments leaked out, and on one occasion when a C-47 force landed it was pulled off the ground by another C-47 equipped with glider snatch gear and towed back to base. The glider snatch technique was used operationally in Europe and South-east Asia. Various marks and variants of the C-47 were built; in order to simplify explanations these are tabulated on page 54, with merely the main variants described in the text.

The first complete change of designation in the military series came with the C-53-DO Skytrooper; built specifically as troop transports at the Douglas Santa Monica factory, they had the same engines as the C-47-DL but did not have large cargo doors or reinforced floors. Twenty-eight troops could be carried and glider towing equipment was fitted. A later variant, the C-53D-DO, had seats along the side of the fuselage. In between these were a batch of eight C-53B-DOs modified for use in the Arctic. They had additional fuel tanks and winter equipment. The designation C-53C-DO was

The XCG-17 glider during tests at Clinton County Army Base in the summer of 1944; it proved to be a practicable proposition but the demand for gliders was then receding and no orders were forthcoming.

Right: GI paratroopers board a C-53 for a practice jump during pre-war exercises, as indicated by the red cross on the fuselage.
Below: A wartime colour photo of USAAF C-47B 43-16299 on a pre-delivery flight. Note the aircraft line number 4152.

Main picture: Douglas Dakota DC-3 (KDC3-F4-1) in mid-flight painted in pre-war colours.

Left to right: Attractively marked USAF C-47A 0-292097 was a visitor to Blackbushe for the 1955 Farnborough Show.
Another Blackbushe visitor to the 1958 Farnborough Show was this Italian Air Force C-47, SM-19.
DC-3 G-AMYW at Croydon in the late 1950s with a curious arrangement above the fuselage, presumably for some type of magnetometer survey work.
R-4D-8 Super Dakota 12437 of the US Navy was converted from an R4D-5. Along with the Convair R4Y-1 141021, it formed part of a static display at RAF West Malling.

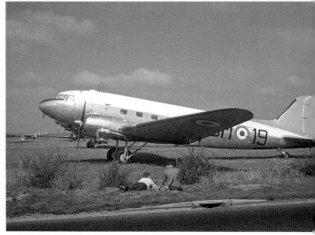

Left above: The Tri-Turbo Three N23SA was the first DC-3 to perform at an SBAC Display when it was shown in September 1978.

Left below: French registered DC-3C-F-BEIF photographed in 1971 fitted with bulged doors to cover the retracted undercarriage, part of a conversion offered in kit form by several companies.

Right above: What can be done with an old DC-3 elegant CF-QCM at Calgary in 1972. Note weather radar nose and 'picture' window, also the highly polished propellers which appear to have extra long shafts.

Right centre: Canadian Armed Forces C-47 12970 at Calgary in February 1971.

Right below: Conroy's Turbo Three N4700C had two Rolls-Royce Dart turboprops when exhibited at the 1969 Paris Air Show. It was later to reappear as the Tri-Turbo Three.

Planes of the Confederate Air Force based at Harlingen in Texas photographed air-to-air in 1977 on display at an air-show.

Above: DC-3 Trans New England N18105 still in service, illustrating the civil aviation authorities' reluctance to replace the tried and trusted Dakota.

Below: The DC-3 was one of a variety of fixed-wing aircraft used by the Royal Canadian Armed Forces' Transport Command in search-and-rescue operations within Canada.

given to a batch of aircraft which had been ordered by airlines but taken over on the production line and completed as military aircraft.

The last series of USAAF aircraft were C-117A-DKs, built in 1945 as staff transports with seating for 21 in airline comfort. The cargo door and reinforced floor were not fitted, but the aircraft were similar in other respects to the C-47B-DK. Like that version, their R-1830-90C engines were fitted with two-stage blowers which also proved unsatisfactory in service, so 11 of the 17 aircraft built had the high blowers removed and were redesignated C-117B-DK. The USAAF took delivery of its last C-117A on 29 December 1945, and this was the last military version of the DC-3 design to be built.

The US Navy and Marine Corps used 568 DC-3 variants under the basic designation R4D, but of these only 78 were direct purchases, the others being diverted from USAAF contracts. The first two aircraft, ex-airline DC-3s, entered service in 1941 as VIP transports under the designation R4D-2F (later R4D-2Z). They had the small doors of the airline version; one was based at Naval Air Station, Pensacola, a new training base, and the other at NAS Anacostia.

Navy R4Ds on transport operations served with Squadrons VR-1, VR-2 and VR-3 of the Naval Air Transport Service, and the South Pacific Combat Air Transport Service, the latter being formed in 1942.

The R4Ds were kept busy flying supplies into combat areas and in a month of operations carried 3.3 million lbs (1.5 million kg) of freight, 941,000 lbs (426,800 kg) of mail and 22,000 passengers, some of these being casualties evacuated. The R4D-3s and -4s were used by the Marine Corps as paratroop transports.

There were a number of variants used for specialised roles (see page 54) and these, together with the transports, served for a number

of years in vital but unspectacular missions. Ironically, it was after the war that Navy R4Ds came into the limelight when they were used to support Antarctic expeditions. In particular, the launching of six R4D-5Ls with jet-assisted take-off from the deck of the aircraft carrier USS *Philippine Sea* on 29 January 1947 in Operation High Jump attracted press publicity and the claim that it was the first occasion on which such large aircraft had been carrier-borne on a major operation. The R4D had a span of 95 ft (29 m) and gross weight of 29,000 lb (13,154 kg) compared with a span of 67 ft 7 in (20.5 m) and gross 31,000 lb (14,062 kg) of the B-25B Mitchells led by Jimmy Doolittle in the famous Tokyo raid of 18 April 1942, launched from the USS *Hornet*. The 16 Mitchells, however, had to contend with a shorter flight deck and did not have the benefits of JATO, but the R4Ds were certainly large aircraft to fly from a carrier deck and operated on the edge of the Antarctic for three weeks under the command of Captain 'Trigger' Hawkes. These were the first USN carrier operations in deep Antarctic waters.

Another Antarctic mission,

Operation Deep Freeze, was undertaken by Captain Hawkes with an R4D-5L, flying 840 miles (1,350 km) from Ross Island and becoming the first aircraft to land at the South Pole, on 31 October 1956, dropping three scientists.

A C-47 had landed at the North Pole on 3 May 1952, in support of the establishment of a weather station, and the DC-3 series therefore became the first to have landed at both Poles.

Operation Deep Freeze, the setting up of a base for civilian scientific teams to study Antarctic conditions, involved a total of 17 R4Ds, of which six were R4D-8s – the Super DC-3, described later.

Returning to the USAAF use of the C-47 series, the formation of that service's Air Transport Command on 1 July 1942 was a major landmark in the aircraft's history, as the C-47 became the ATC's backbone. Shortly afterwards, Troop Carrier Command was formed, but prior to this the 316th Troop Carrier Group

The cockpit of C-47-DL 41-18672, photographed in November 1942. On the original print it is possible to see a placard saying 'single engine absolute ceiling 11,000 feet'.

had been formed on 14 February 1942 at Patterson Field, Ohio. This Group was to see considerable action in Europe.

One of the first ATC tasks was in Asia. With the fall of Burma and Malaya to the Japanese, following the loss of the Philippines and Netherlands East Indies, it became imperative to open an aerial supply route to China from India. China had been at war with Japan since July 1937, and a large number of Japanese troops were involved in the struggle. While they were tied down there they could not be used elsewhere in the Asian theatre and it was therefore in the Allies' interest to support China.

The China-Burma-India theatre had primarily involved British and Chinese forces in its ground and air operations but an American commitment to support China necessitated the formation of the United States 10th Air Force in February 1942 at Patterson Field, Ohio. From a modest beginning with a few bombers and fighters, the 10th was gradually built up and the planning of a transport service began.

At that time the China National Aviation Corporation, a Sino-American company, owned 45 per cent by Pan American Airlines and 55 per cent by the Chinese Government, was operating between Calcutta and Kunming. Prior to the Japanese attack on Pearl Harbor, CNAC flew regular scheduled services from Hong Kong to Chungking, then to Rangoon and Calcutta with DC-2s and -3s, and the airline pioneered trans-Himalayas flights between Assam and Chungking. 'Over the Hump' flights were to become one of the great achievements of the war, since it was necessary to fly above 25,000 ft (7,620 m) to clear the mountains in this region, universally recognised as one of the most dangerous flying areas anywhere in the world. Much of the country was unexplored and uncharted; where the mountains ended thick forests began and when the monsoons came ground

and air conditions were appalling.

With the supply of ten C-47s to CNAC the airline was able to enlarge its operations and continued to operate in parallel with the Air Force.

Two Commands were established within the 10th Air Force; the Trans-India Ferry Command was tasked with moving cargo between Karachi and Assam, while the Assam-Burma-China Ferry Command handled that route. The latter was established at Dinjan using three C-47s plus ten DC-3s impressed from Pan American and began operations

with the haulage of 30,000 gallons (113,562 litres) of aviation fuel and 500 gallons (1,893 litres) of lubricants to China. This was intended to enable Doolittle's B-25s engaged in the Tokyo mission to refuel in China and fly on to India but all the B-25s crashed in China so the fuel was not needed.

The war in Burma was going badly for the Allies, and the C-47s were kept busy with deliveries of ammunition, fuel and supplies, bringing out civilians and wounded troops on the return journey. As the situation deteriorated further,

the 10th Air Force aircraft became busier with evacuation and brought out 4,499 passengers plus 900 tons of cargo between April and June 1942, while RAF aircraft evacuated 4,117 people and CNAC almost 10,000. The C-47s, built to carry 24 passengers, were regularly carrying 50 or more at heights of up to 18,000 ft (5,485 m), 50 per cent above their designed maximum altitude.

Supply drops to the retreating Allied troops included some 2,000 tons (2,032 tonnes) of rice, salt and medicine to the Chinese troops who were in a very poor

state. While this was going on, the American Joint Chiefs of Staff in Washington were having difficulties in procuring aircraft for the proposed 'Hump' route, but eventually 25 DC-3s were impressed from US airlines to begin the operation. Crews were obtained by recalling 100 airline pilots with reserve commissions and the 1st Ferrying Group formed at Morrison Field, Florida. Since all crews had extreme flying experience, briefing was limited to long-range, over-water flying, and the aircraft were flown out from Florida via Brazil, West Africa and

Above left: The sole YC-47C amphibian, 42-92577 was converted from a C-47A.

Top: C-47A 43-15422 of the US Signal Corps at Mindoro. Some type of marking on the nose appears to have been censored.

Above: Built as a C-47B, 43-48906 was one of eight aircraft subsequently modified for the USAAF as C-47Es by Pan American for airways checking. The changes included installation of 1,290-hp Pratt & Whitney R-2000-4 engines.

the Middle East to India in April and May, 1942.

There were considerable difficulties in the 'Hump' operations, many of these resulting from personal differences between the various commanders, but this

has no part of the C-47 story. Suffice to say that the aircraft proved itself in conditions far exceeding those for which it had been designed and in weather which would have destroyed many other aircraft. Crosswinds of up to 150 mph (240 km/h), severe icing, turbulence, up and down draughts, which could push an aircraft up 12,000 ft (3,660 m) one minute and take it back the next, were almost commonplace. There were instances when the weight of ice on the wings was sufficient to warp them and aircraft dropped thousands of feet before the ice was melted by the higher temperatures at lower altitudes. It was often necessary to fly on instruments throughout the trip and a number of aircraft were lost when they crashed into mountains, some as a result of Japanese deception stations putting out a false DF bearing.

While the flying conditions were awful, ground conditions in the monsoon period were atrocious; between May and October in Assam 200 in (500 cm) of rain fell, so only paved runways and hardstandings remained operational. Even then, an airfield had to close when the water on the runways reached nine inches (23 cm) deep so that it could be drained. Assam was also notorious for its heavy ground fogs which caused a number of crashes and in fact the weather proved a worse enemy than the Japanese. There is a case on record of the loss of nine aircraft in one storm on the 'Hump' run and such was the strain on crews that flying time was counted as official combat flying time; up to 1943, 80 per cent of decorations awarded to the ATC went to crews of the India-China Wing.

In addition to the C-47s, C-46 Commandos, C-54 Skymasters and C-87 Liberator transports were used. From 1943 the C-46 began to come into service but suffered a number of technical problems for some time, including a disturbing tendency to explode or crash. These were eventually solved, and the C-46 with its one-third greater capacity, higher speed and ceiling began to replace the C-47s.

Maintenance was always a problem in the South-East Asia theatre; high humidity created rusting of metal and rotting of rubber components, dust in the dry season was an ever-present enemy to engines and mud in the wet season was an enemy to everything and everybody. Extremes of heat – up to 150°F (65°C) in the shade – made metal too hot to touch, requiring most maintenance to be undertaken at night. For major maintenance and repair, the 10th Air Force's Air Service Command had two depots, one at Agra which mainly serviced C-46s and some C-47s, while at Bangalore the depot was the Hindustan Aircraft Corporation's factory, the best facility in India. By the end of the war, 650,000 tons (660,000 tonnes) of supplies had been airlifted over the 'Hump', and of this more than half was carried in 1945 but it had been achieved at a high cost in crews and aircraft. The RAF participated to a lesser degree in flying the 'Hump' route from May 1943, when crews from No 31 Squadron were seconded to CNAC for route training, regular flights beginning in August.

Left: An early post-war scene at Croydon; AB Aerotransport's DC-3A SE-BAB, an original purchase from Fokker in August 1937, shares the tarmac with a Bloch 220, delivered to Air France at about the same time.

Top: An unidentified XC-47C 'on the step'. At least four such aircraft are believed to have been built.

Above left: This C-47B 43-49071 appears to be an ex-Lease-Lend aircraft now in Russian civil markings and has a single door on the starboard side.

Above right: Russian built Li-2 No. 206 of the Hungarian Air Force at Budapest/Budaors Airport in the late 1970s.

Right: Czechoslovak Air Force Dakotas were frequent visitors to Croydon in the early post-war years. D-23 is shown.

Bottom right: During a South American demonstration tour, a Dart Herald met up with a Brazilian Air Force C-47.

Dakotas

Delivery of the first C-47 to the RAF took place at Douglas' Long Beach factory on 9 January 1943, and the type was christened Dakota, the name by which all C-47s and DC-3s have been universally known ever since. The second Dakota arrived at Prestwick in the hands of RAF Ferry Command on 11 February.

The RAF operated 21 DC-2s and 8 DC-3s following their impressment for military service; the Dakotas received totalled 1,920 of four different marks which corresponded to USAAF variants – 53 Mk.1s (C-47), 9 Mk.2s (C-53), 962 Mk.3s (C-47A) and 896 Mk.4s (C-47B). All were supplied under Lease-Lend and equipped no less than 25 squadrons during the war, 15 in the UK and 10 overseas. Post-war operations were undertaken by 13 squadrons, and another 9 squadrons used them during the Berlin Airlift.

The impressed DC-2s and -3s were operated by Nos. 31 and 117 Squadrons and mention has previously been made of RAF use of the DC-2. The DC-3s were a mixed batch including two each from Eastern Air Lines and American Air Lines and one from Capital Airlines, the source of the others being unrecorded. All served in the India-Burma theatre and were either destroyed by enemy action or eventually struck off charge; three survived long enough to serve with Indian National Airways.

The newly-delivered RAF Dakotas were soon in action in Burma, dropping supplies for the British forces, operating at times without fighter cover since they were often beyond the range of British fighters but in one ten-day period they flew 177 supply sorties by day and night without loss. On one occasion an RAF Dakota landed on an 800 yard (732 m) strip to bring out 17 casualties impossible to save by other means. The pilot, Flying Officer Vlasto, was awarded the DFC for this operation.

A vast programme of airfield construction was undertaken in which the Dakotas played their part – a heavy bomber field, for instance, required 300,000 tons (305,000 tonnes) of concrete, or 200 tons (203 tonnes) of bituminised hessian, or 600 Dakota loads of steel planking (PSP). The scale of construction can be gauged by the fact that the number of airfields rose from four with all-weather runways in March 1942 to 285 completed by the end of the 1943 monsoon season. Of these, 45 were handed over to the USAAF and that service was also given facilities at RAF airfields.

Needless to say, the RAF strength in aircraft grew in proportion to the airfield growth, and as far as the Dakotas were concerned their numbers rose from 29 to 100. It says much for the efforts of the transport crews

that, according to *Wings of the Phoenix* – the official story of the air war in Burma – the greatest aid which tactical aircraft rendered in Burma was in their support and

Two of the six US Navy R4Ds (the nearest is R4D-5 17101) aboard the USS *Philippine Sea* from which they took off in Operation High Jump, supporting an Antarctic Survey Team in 1947.

protection of the Dakotas, since without these no military defence could have lasted long.

It was generally realised that probably the hardest worker in a Dakota drop was the 'kicker'. During the period when the aircraft was over the dropping zone and after the dispatchers had placed the loads in neat piles, the 'kickers' would lie flat on their back with feet braced against the base of the load and shoulders pushing on the opposite wall. On a signal from the pilot, the 'kicker' thrust with his feet while the dispatchers helped the load out. Apart from being hot work, it was dangerous in the turbulence often encountered at low altitude.

In March 1944, the Dakotas were to feature in their biggest mission to date, carrying 10,000 troops over the Japanese forces into the back areas where they could cut the enemy's supply lines. After some initial changes when it was suspected that the Japanese knew of the plan, 80 Waco CC-4A Hadrian gliders were towed off at dusk and experienced heavy turbulence which caused several cables to break, but the majority of gliders reached their objective only to find ruts in the landing area which caused a number to crash. However, by dint of much hard work, the landing area was cleared and the next night Dakotas flew in with supplies which included mules. On the single strip operations proceeded at a rate of one take-off or one landing every three minutes, with 62 Dakotas landing in the hours of darkness.

Dakotas were to see much action in Burma, not the least of which concerned rescue missions which were shared with light aircraft such as L-5 Sentinels, Tiger Moths and Fox Moths. On one occasion a Dakota pilot was credited with a 'kill' when an Oscar fighter collided with the transport's tail and lost a wing.

Meanwhile, other RAF Dakotas were being employed in the Mediterranean theatre. No 4 Middle East Training School,

Tests were carried out on several types of aircraft in France during the 1950s with small underwing jets to improve take-off performance. This French Air Force C-47 has two Turbomeca Palas turbojets.

formed in 1942 as a parachute unit, moved to Haifa in March 1943 and was helped by a USAAF squadron of C-47s and C-53s until its own aircraft were available. Dakotas began to re-equip No 216 Squadron in March 1943, replacing Lockheed Hudsons, and a flight of their aircraft in the following three months carried out many training and several operational sorties, including the dropping of Greek paratroops during the Aegean campaign. The Allied invasion of Sicily was shared by the British 8th and American 7th Armies, and the first airborne attack in the British sector on the night of 9/10 July 1943 was undertaken by 137 gliders towed by Halifaxes, Albemarles and C-47s, the latter numbering 109 and comprising four-fifths of the tug force. The tugs were not to approach the coast nearer than 3,000 yards (2,790 m) and winds made the operation difficult, many gliders parting prematurely from their tugs and nearly 50 coming down in the sea with the loss of their troops. Only 12 gliders reached their objective, a road bridge. The American force was also widely scattered and could not be counted a success, while five nights later the parachute battalions took their turn in a fleet of 135 aircraft and

19 gliders; of the former, 105 were USAAF C-47s. Heavy anti-aircraft fire caused the loss of 14 aircraft including 10 C-47s and 19 aircraft returned to base with paratroops still on board.

While these operations were being carried out, plans were being laid for Operation Overlord, the Allies' return to French soil. This was to take place on 6 June 1944, by which time the RAF had received a large number of its Dakotas. Five squadrons, under the control of No 46 Group (Nos 48, 233, 271, 512 and 575), contributed 108 Dakotas to carry the main group of the 3rd Parachute Brigade to Normandy, and to tow Horsa gliders to the battle areas, while other aircraft of Nos 38 and 46 Groups carried the 5th Parachute Brigade. A total of 4,310 paratroops were dropped while the gliders flew in another 493. Losses were seven tugs and 22 gliders. The two Groups were in action again at the end of D-Day when a further 256 gliders were towed across the Channel with reinforcements and supplies for the troops landed earlier.

The USAAF made a giant

contribution to D-Day with 14 Groups of the 9th Air Force Troop Carrier Command carrying men of the 82nd and 101st Airborne Division. A total of 821 C-47s and C-53s carried troops, while a further 104 towed Hadrian gliders. This mighty armada used 14 airfields and the first aircraft to leave – from Greenham Common – were taking off at intervals of 11 seconds from 22.48 hrs on 5 June. They crossed the Channel at only 500 ft (152 m) in a 10-mile (16-km) wide corridor, climbing to 1,500 ft (457 m) in the area of the Channel Islands, descending again to 700 ft (213 m) and 110 mph (177 km/h) for the drop, which began at 00.16 on 6 June. Twenty-two hours later the resupply column of 408 tugs all towing Horsa gliders were over the drop zone (in general the Horsas operated by day and the Hadrians by night), and the following morning 320 C-47s and C-53s returned to the zone with further supplies.

During the period USAAF losses totalled 46 troop carriers, and a further 449 were damaged. The American C-47s were in action again on the night of 14/15 August when 400 aircraft carried paratroops to Southern France to prepare landing fields for 407 gliders by the next morning. A total of 9,000 airborne troops were ferried together with their equipment and ammunition and on 15 August beach landings by Allied troops near Cannes met with only light resistance.

The next major operation in Europe involving the Dakota was the ill-fated airborne landings around Arnhem in September 1944. Much has been written about Operation Market Garden and it is not proposed to repeat this in great detail here, but merely to cover briefly the Dakota's part.

The purpose of the operation was to capture vital bridges in the areas of Arnhem and Nijmegen to facilitate a swift advance into Germany, and the first air lift on 17 September consisted of 320 tugs with gliders. Bad weather en route caused the loss of 35 gliders but the loads of 21 were recovered. In all, around 500 gliders took off for Arnhem on that day; on the following day, another 296 tugs and gliders were despatched, one Dakota being lost.

The battle did not go well for the Allies and German resistance was considerably fiercer than had been expected since there were many more German troops in the area than intelligence reports had suggested. Supplies for the now surrounded Allied troops continued to be dropped by aircraft, many of them Dakotas and the statistics of the operations carried out between 17 and 30 September make interesting reading. A total of 20,190 troops had been parachuted in, a further 13,781 had been carried by gliders and 905 were landed on a small strip cut by the early arrivals. Equipment and supplies weighing 5,230 tons (5,314 tonnes), 1,927 vehicles and 568 artillery weapons had been airfreighted in and Nos 38 and 46 Group, RAF, had lost 55 aircraft, while another 327 were damaged; many of these were Dakotas and a number of decorations for gallantry were awarded, including the supreme award – the Victoria Cross. The recipient was Flight Lieutenant David Lord, Captain of a Dakota of No 271 Squadron based at Down Ampney.

Lord's aircraft was one of 17 carrying ammunition panniers to be dropped on the outskirts of Arnhem and nearing the target at 1,500 ft (457 m) it came under heavy anti-aircraft fire, being hit twice in the wing and having its starboard engine set on fire. With only three minutes to go before the drop, and with the engine ablaze, Lord descended to 900 ft (274 m) and came under even heavier fire. Damage to the roller track in the Dakota caused the panniers to jam and the crew had to manhandle them out through the doorway. The delay thus caused resulted in two panniers still being in position at the end of the run, so Lord took the aircraft round for a second run over the drop zone; by now at only 600 ft (183 m) and well ablaze the Dakota was being shot to pieces but Lord held it straight and ordered the crew to bail out. Before they could do so the wing detached, one crew member was propelled through the door to parachute safely down and the Dakota crashed with no survivors. The posthumous award of the VC was gazetted in November 1945.

The last airborne assault of the war was Operation Varsity, undertaken on 24 March 1945, to secure bridgeheads across the Rhine. The transport aircraft and gliders were operating from England and from bases around Paris and Rheims; in some cases C-47s towed two Waco Hadrians.

Six parachute battalions of the British 6th Airborne Division emplaned in 242 C-47s of the USAAF 52nd Wing flying from airfields in Essex, while the American 17th Airborne Division were carried in 1,155 C-47s and C-46s and 908 gliders from French airfields. The RAF's No 38 Group supplied Stirlings and Halifaxes, and No 46 Group Dakotas, for towing 381 Horsas and Hamilcars from England, the Dakotas being used for the lighter Horsas.

In general, Operation Varsity went well although as in other operations a few gliders were lost through heavy turbulence but many more were destroyed by enemy fire. The two RAF Groups lost seven tugs while the Americans lost 58 with a further 352 damaged. It has been suggested that the considerable difference in loss ratios was probably attributable to the differences in glider release height – the RAF released at 2,500 ft (762 m) while the USAAF chose 600 ft (183 m).

Dakotas were used on a number of occasions for clandestine flights into enemy territory, and some into Poland are worthy of mention. In April 1944 an aircraft of No 267

Brand-new C-47-DL 41-18604 poses on 14 October 1940, in front of an impressive collection of wing sections.

Squadron based at Bari, Italy carried out a 1,600 mile (2,575 km) night round trip to Poland to pick up five passengers and documents, and the squadron repeated the operation the following month. However, the third trip, made in July, was the most eventful. With the long summer evenings it was necessary to fly part of the way in daylight and on reaching the landing area, a muddy field, the Dakota made a safe landing. It was soon loaded with a valuable cargo of information on V weapons and some parts obtained by the Poles following crashes of the weapons, but extreme difficulty was encountered when the time came for take off from the soggy surface and the Dakota was on the ground for some time before it was finally freed from the muddy embrace and staggered into the air at 65 mph (105 km/h).

A noteworthy Dakota flight was made in June 1943 when an RAF aircraft towed a Hadrian glider across the Atlantic from west to east, the first time such a feat had been attempted. Since this was a very unusual operation it is worth recounting. Air Chief Marshal Sir Frederick Bowhill, in charge of the North and South Atlantic Bomber Ferry which delivered aircraft from Canada to the Allied Commands in Europe and Africa, put forward the idea of a transatlantic air freighter service using gliders for carrying freight from west to east and carrying ferry crews back after they had made their deliveries. The opinions of the ferry crews on this suggestion are, perhaps fortunately, not recorded, but the scheme was considered worthy of trial.

To provide an additional safety factor, the glider and tug would be accompanied by a Catalina flying boat on a normal delivery flight so that it could, in theory, land and pick up the crews if necessary. In practice, extensive ice packs and turbulent seas would have made this virtually impossible; fortunately it was not put to the test.

The Hadrian had two types of undercarriage – one a conventional type with wheels and brakes, while the other, a tactical version, had no brakes and could be dropped when airborne, landing being made on underbelly skids. The latter gear was selected as being safer in case a ditching was necessary. The towrope was 350 ft (107 m) long, made of 11/16 in pure nylon, and had a stretch under load of 1 in 10. It had a breaking strength of 800 lbs (363 kg).

The Dakota tug selected for the crossing had its 850 gallon (3,864 l) fuel capacity increased by long-range tanks to 1,800 gallons (8,183 l) and its initial tow speed was 120 mph (193 km/h) for the first 4½ hours, increasing to 140 mph (225 km/h) as the fuel was used. Maximum permissible speed for the glider under tow was 150 mph (240 km/h). When ready for flight, the Dakota's normal all-up weight was increased from 22,500 lb to 31,500 lb (10,200-14,290 kg).

A number of practice flights were undertaken culminating in the setting up of a new world's non-stop record of 1,187 miles (1,911 km) from Nassau to Richmond, Virginia, in 8 hours 50 minutes.

23 June 1943 was a fine, sunny day and the Dakota/Hadrian combination took off from Montreal to set course for the first leg to Goose Bay. The first half of the flight was uneventful, but from then on severe turbulence was encountered over Labrador, with temperatures below zero, and instrument flying was necessary at times. At Goose Bay, the glider cast off at 1,000 ft (305 m) and landed. The first suitable weather for the next leg came on 27 June, when the aircraft took off for

Above: An interesting line-up of C-47Bs for the USAAF, RAF (KK131), Russia (line number 3431) and China.

Right: DC-3 ZS-JMP of Avex Air was operated on aerial survey work, hence the various aerials on the top of the fuselage, the MAD boom protruding from the rear and the magnetometer 'bomb' beneath the fuselage. It was seen at Rand Airport, Johannesburg, in 1977.

Below: Dakota 3 TS423 has been an experimental aircraft for most of its post-war life. Coming from 436 Squadron, RCAF, it was operated by Scottish Aviation on behalf of Ferranti from August 1949, joining the Ferranti Flying Unit when it was formed in June 1953. Used for a number of radar projects with nose radomes, it passed briefly to Elliotts at West Malling in October 1963 and later to RAE at West Freugh. It is currently based at Duxford as G-DAKS.

Greenland, the first long leg over the ocean. It proved uneventful apart from some slight icing, most of the flight being above cloud.

Following a complete equipment check, the flight resumed on 30 June and after a rather frightening take off when the Dakota used all the runway, the combination had to circle to gain sufficient height for the crossing of the 12,000 ft (3,658 m) Greenland ice cap. Bumpy conditions were encountered and instrument flying was again necessary. For the glider crew the next hour was a frightening one, since the tug disappeared in cloud and only about 30 ft (9 m) of the towrope was visible; flying with the degree of accuracy required to maintain position relative to the Dakota in

The US Federal Aviation Administration used a number of DC-3s post-war. N70 is illustrated.

such conditions was extremely tiring but the combination gradually succeeded in climbing out of cloud at 11,500 ft (3,500 m). Several hours later a safe landing was made at Reykjavik, Iceland, the glider landing one minute after the Catalina put down in the Bay.

After repairs to the towrope, the final leg from Reykjavik to Prestwick, Scotland, was flown on 1 July. Probably the most terrifying part of the flight was running into a balloon barrage in Scotland which necessitated a steep climbing turn during which the Dakota passed over the glider travelling in the opposite direction!

A number of valuable lessons had been learned from the flight and as a result of these it was decided that such glider trains were not really practicable. Apart from the experience, the journey was not wasted since the Hadrian carried a full cargo of radio, aircraft and motor parts and vaccine for Russia. The end of the war in Europe saw Dakotas heavily involved in the return of troops to the UK, and the type was still operational in the Far East.

However, the peace did not mark the end of the Dakota's service career and it continued operating in most parts of the world. In June 1948 British security forces were engaged in detecting and destroying Communist guerillas terrorising Malayan villages and disrupting production in the tin mines and at rubber plantations. Operation Firedog involved a wide variety of RAF aircraft, Royal Navy Seafires and Fireflies, and Army Austers before it was finally wound up after 12 years in October 1960. Not surprisingly, the Dakota took an active part in Firedog from the beginning, when No 110 Squadron moved from its base at Changi, Singapore to Kuala Lumpur, Malaya.

No 110 was one of three Dakota squadrons forming the Transport Wing at Changi (the others being 48 and 52), normally operating as a military airline linking Singapore and Malaya to other parts of Burma. Their role in Firedog was supply-dropping to troops in the jungle hunting terrorists. This seemingly innocuous task was, in fact, difficult and at times hazardous, with drops into small clearings hacked out of the jungle, often in conditions of bad weather and poor visibility. In November 1948, 110 was relieved by 52 Squadron which, in the six months it was based at Kuala Lumpur, dropped almost 180 tons (183 tonnes) of supplies, carried 2,300 passengers and 80 tons (81 tonnes) of freight. Next came 48 Squadron and the work was stepped up; by the time the Dakotas had been replaced by Valettas in May 1951 the former had delivered 3,500 tons (3,550 tonnes) of supplies to the security forces. The RAF Dakota crews underwent conversion to the Valetta and during this time Dakotas of the RAAF and RNZAF continued the good work.

The Dakota's final job in Firedog, performed by the last three aircraft in squadron service (No 267 Squadron) and shared with Austers, consisted of low flying, as slowly as possible, and using loud hailers to pass messages to the terrorists, a form of psychological warfare. The three Dakotas, named Faith, Hope and Charity also operated in and out of jungle strips on casualty evacuation until November 1958 when No 267 was re-numbered 209 Squadron and disbanded for four years, reforming at Benson with Armstrong Whitworth Argosys.

Operational flying of another kind for the RAF Dakotas and USAF C-47s came in 1948. On 24 June the Russians, in an attempt to force the other occupying powers out of Berlin, set up a blockade closing all roads, railways and waterways leading from West Germany through the Russian zone to Berlin, cutting off West Berlin's supply of food, fuel, medicines and other vital supplies.

Allied reaction was swift; the only avenue of transport left open was the air, via three 20-mile (32-km) wide corridors and on 26 June the USAF European Command, ordered to establish an airlift, flew 25 C-47s into Tempelhof Airport, in the American Zone, with food and coal. It had been calculated that a minimum of 1,500 tons (1,520 tonnes) of supplies per day would be needed to maintain life in West Berlin, a tonnage far beyond the capabilities of the number of C-47s available. The USAF therefore hurriedly brought in some 300 C-54 Skymasters to their West German bases, notably at Frankfurt/ Rheinmain, while British Dakotas, Yorks, Lancastrians and even

Sunderland flying boats joined the lift, christened Operation Plainfare but forever known as the Berlin Airlift. By 15 July the aircraft had reached a daily tonnage of 1,530 tons (1,555 tonnes), proving that the minimum required could be achieved.

The demands of the airlift led to RAF Transport Command cancelling most of its scheduled services and all its training flights and a number of Dakotas in storage at Maintenance Units were rapidly brought back into service. To speed up refurbishment of the stored Dakotas civilian contractors were employed including Scottish Aviation at Prestwick, Airwork at Southampton, Fields at Tollerton and Marshalls of Cambridge. Several squadrons which had been disbanded were reformed and the first RAF Dakotas of 72 flown to Germany flew from Wunstorf to Berlin on 28 June. A total of 50 Dakotas and 43 Yorks were based at Wunstorf which was then operating to capacity. Even this became too much and the Dakotas moved to Fassberg where they were mainly used for transporting coal from the Ruhr, an unpleasant change from the previous loads of hay, flour and food. In September the USAF C-54s moved into Fassberg displacing the Dakotas

which took up residence at Lubeck and resumed food flights. The RAF Dakotas had been operating into Gatow, Berlin's military airfield in the British Zone, but in November 1948 a new airfield at Tegel in the French Zone was opened, completed in only three months, and for several weeks the Dakotas used this until their return to Gatow. A very rigid air traffic control system was initiated, to keep the aircraft flowing in and out of Berlin. There was no room for errors in approach or landing since at peak periods an aircraft was landing every three minutes; a missed approach meant that the offending aircraft had to return to its West German base without landing and get another slot since there was no room for a circuit. The Russians ended the blockade on 12 May, but the lift continued until September to build up the city's stocks of food and coal. In all, the airlift totalled 277,000 flights, an average of 700 a day, and carried 2.3 million tons of supplies. At the time the blockade ended it was estimated that the lift had cost $170 million; seventy-five airmen died while on missions.

In June 1950, North Korean troops invaded South Korea, which was supported by the USA, and the war which was to last for three

years had begun. Once again, the C-47 was in action, evacuating personnel and supply dropping, and on 20 October 1950, a force of 40 C-47s and 71 C-119s dropped paratroops and 300 tons of supplies to the hard-pressed South Koreans. Later, C-47s evacuated 4,689 troops of the US 1st Marine Division who had been trapped.

Some aircraft were converted to RC-47Ds and operated in support of Douglas B-26 Invaders engaged on night bombing missions, dropping flares to illuminate the targets. A few R4D-8s were used for the same purpose.

Also operating in the Korean theatre were C-47s of the Royal Hellenic Air Force, attached to the USAF 21st Troop Carrier Squadron, while the RAAF's No 86 Transport Wing based in Japan maintained a scheduled service to Australian personnel fighting in Korea. Korean National Airlines flew a limited service with DC-3s to and from Japan.

In 1961 the war in Vietnam began. Never officially declared, the 'war' lasted for 11 years, with

An elegant US Army SC-47K at Love Field, Dallas, on 27 July 1966. Note undercarriage doors; colour scheme was white and red with black trim.

the North Vietnamese regime and Communist-backed Vietminh seeking to overthrow the South Vietnamese government. The south was supported by the USA while the USSR actively backed the north. Thousands of aircraft were involved in the conflict and once again the C-47 was recalled to operations.

A number of types were used for reconnaissance missions, even some RC-47s, but a completely new variant appeared, the AC-47. The US forces were experiencing difficulties in attacking enemy troops at night and it was considered that a gunship version

of the C-47 would fill the bill. Some C-47s were equipped with three rapid firing 7.62 mm guns each of which was capable of firing 6,000 rounds per minute from large ammunition boxes which occupied much of the fuselage.

The method of attack was simple; when a target was identified, usually a besieged village, the pilot sighted by pointing the left wing at it, lining up with an optional sight in the left cockpit window. The AC-47 went into a banked turn to the left and the guns opened up from three of the cabin windows, either firing blind or with the aid of a

searchlight. Flares could also be dropped, each of 24 million candlepower. The AC-47s were so successful that similar conversions were carried out on Fairchild C-119s and Lockheed C-130E Hercules. USAF EC-47s with electronic jamming equipment also operated in South Vietnam and that country's air force had a number of C-47s on strength. Some civilian-owned DC-3s were also involved and one, belonging to Continental Air Services, created a record on 23 March 1975, when it lifted 98 orphans and five attendants from Du Lat to Saigon; the aircraft had a crew of three.

Manufacture abroad

In March 1934, Nakajima in Japan paid $80,000 for the manufacturing rights of the DC-2 and the design was adapted to Japanese production methods; a Douglas-built example was delivered to Dai Nippon Airways in December 1934.

The first Nakajima-assembled DC-2 from Douglas components flew in February 1936 with 730 hp Wright Cyclone SGR-1820F2 engines and it was followed by five similarly powered models (later re-engined with SGR-1820-F52s) for Greater Japan Air Lines. The first aircraft was impressed for service with the Japanese Army.

Experience with the DC-2 made it inevitable that Japan would be interested in the DC-3, and 20 were imported between November 1937 and February 1939 for Dai Nippon Airways, 13 with Cyclone engines and seven with Twin Wasps. They served through the Pacific War until the survivors were scrapped.

In February 1938, Mitsui acquired DC-3 manufacturing rights for $90,000 and bought two unassembled DC-3s on instructions from the Japanese Navy. Two companies, Showa Hikoko Kogyo and Nakajima Hikoki, were selected to undertake production and Showa delivered the first two prototypes (the US manufactured pair) in October 1939 and April 1940. These were designated L2D1 and had 1,000 hp Pratt & Whitney SB3G

Above left: Camouflaged AC-47 0-48801 seen at Miami was one of 26 aircraft modified in the USA.

Left: Blotchy-camouflaged AC-47 43-48499 with one of its doors removed and a crewman at the ready.

Right: Built by Showa in Japan, the L2D4 and L2D4-1 respectively passenger and cargo transports. Both had a small dorsal turret and extra glazing behind the flight deck.

engines, but production model L2D2s had 1,000 hp Mitsubishi Kinsei 43 engines.

Nakajima delivered 71 aircraft as Navy Type 0 Transport Model 11s between 1940 and 1942, and from that date Showa built the type exclusively. The first sub-variant was the L2D2-1 with a reinforced cargo floor and cargo doors like the C-47; the main production version was the L2D3 (Navy Type 0, Transport Model 22). This was a personnel transport with 1,300 hp Kinsei radials, the L2D3a being similar but with a different mark of engine. Their two equivalent cargo transport versions were respectively the L2D3-1 and -1a.

Armed personnel and cargo transports, respectively L2D4 and D4-1, had a dorsal turret with 13 mm machine gun and two hand-held 7.7 mm guns in fuselage hatches, although these were experimental versions. The final variant, the L2D5 (Navy Type 0, Transport Model 33) was a version of the L2D4 using wood or steel in place of light alloys with 1,560 hp Kinsei radials. It was being built when the war ended and presumably was never completed. Total production in Japan was 487, of which 416 were built by Showa and 71 by Nakajima.

Russia was a prodigious user of the Dakota; 21 DC-3s were bought before the war and licence production rights were negotiated. In 1938, Boris Lisunov went to Douglas' Santa Monica factory for almost two years to study

production methods, then returned home to adapt the type to Russian manufacture and requirements, particularly cold-weather operation. The Russian-built aircraft had their entry door on the starboard side and the engines were initially 900 hp M-62s (licence-built Wright Cyclones) with slotted cold weather baffles. They had a slightly smaller wing area and reduced power which meant less maximum speed but an increased range. Initially designated PS-84, the aircraft were redesignated Lisunov Li-2 in September 1942 in recognition of Lisunov's work on the design; they were later fitted with ASh-62 engines of higher power. First production aircraft came from a Moscow factory but production was transferred to Tashkent in 1941 and more than 2,000 were built between 1940 and 1945. Additionally, the Russians were supplied with 707 C-47s under lease-lend but none of these were returned to the West after the war.

Li-2s were built in a number of versions, as passenger or cargo transports (Li-2P or Li-2G respectively), as mixed passenger/cargo transports (Li-2PG), and as high-altitude transports (Li-2V). Some aircraft were fitted with dorsal gun turrets and wartime use included landing partisans behind the German lines. Post-war, the aircraft continued in service for many years and formed the foundations of new airlines in a number of Communist bloc countries.

An early post-war photograph showing
some of the KLM Airlines' ex-military C-47s
in various stages of conversion to the new
colour scheme worn by PH-TDU.

Post-war service

In Europe too the DC-3 was the staple transport as airlines which had ceased operations when war broke out struggled to rebuild their routes. Surplus C-47s, C-53s and Dakotas were snapped up and it was quite common to see aircraft with their military marks roughly obliterated and temporary registration scrawled on in whitewash for ferry flights from service maintenance units to new owners. Virtually every European country used the DC-3 post-war and Swissair, which had to cease operations eventually when it was surrounded by warring nations, actually restored its routes with two DC-2s and four DC-3s, all bought before the war, but these had to be supplemented by some ex-USAF C-47s. Swissair DC-3s remained in service until the mid-1960s when the final three were handed over to SLS, the company's flying school; one of these is now exhibited in the Swiss Transport Museum in Lucerne. It should be mentioned that Douglas built a few DC-3s after the war ended from incompleted C-117 airframes. The first batch of 28 were designated DC-3Ds and were new aircraft; a further 21 DC-3Cs were rebuilt C-47s, the last of which was delivered in March 1947. The 10,000th aircraft in the DC-3 family had been delivered to the USAAF on 5 May 1945.

Britain's first civilian use of the DC-3 came during the war when five KLM aircraft managed to escape the German invasion and were used by BOAC on services between Bristol and Lisbon. Portugal was, of course, neutral and it was often possible to see British and German DC-3s (captured examples) on the tarmac together. Supplementing the KLM aircraft were six Dakotas diverted from the RAF in March 1943, and

BOAC together with BEA operated a large Dakota fleet for some years, the BEA aircraft later being given the class name Pionair when they were modernised by Scottish Aviation in 1950 and fitted out as 32-seaters.

Use of Dakotas in Britain, however, was not restricted to the State airlines and, in fact, the first British civil conversion was carried out on a C-47A in 1945 by Scottish Aviation who used it on services which included Iceland. A further glut came in 1952 when the RAF disposed of its surviving Dakota 4s which were acquired by a number of charter and internal operators. Several were used for aerial survey work, notably by Fairey Air Surveys while Hunting Aerosurveys had one aircraft with a strutted aerial system above the fuselage for geophysical survey.

While the airline DC-3s in Europe continue to fly the occasional route with companies such as Air Atlantique the military have been just as reluctant to part with the last of their C-47s, odd examples still being around in the 80s. Finland used about ten for some years until a fatal crash decided the government that it was time to replace them but one of the Finnish Air Force aircraft has been acquired by the Dutch Dakota Association which plans to keep it airworthy.

In the USA the DC-3s still flying are all used by small companies; during the 1970s Mohawk Airlines decided on a novel approach to promote the old DC-3s it still owned and launched a 'Gaslight' service with the aircraft interiors redecorated in Edwardian styling, a fashion also adopted for the stewardesses' uniform.

Since the 1950s manufacturers have tried to design a DC-3 replacement; the Nord 262 was probably the first to approach the

problem seriously, but the difficulty lay not so much in designing a 30-seat aircraft as in airlines finding the money to afford new aircraft. The present spate of new airliners in this class – Shorts 330 and 360, Saab-Fairchild SF340, Embraer Brasilia, de Havilland Canada Dash 8 and the slightly larger CASA-Nurtanio CN-235 and Aerospatiale/Aeritalia ATR 42 give a wide range of choice and surely the DC-3 cannot go on for ever . . . can it?

Left: The leased DC-2 'Uiver' that re-enacted the London to Melbourne race in 1984.

Below left: Nordair DC-3C CF-IQR, at Montreal/Dorval on 1 February 1970, had skis with auxiliary aerofoils at the rear.

Top: Portuguese Air Force C-47A 6151, one of about 60 used. All remaining were taken out of service in 1976 for breaking up or disposal.

Right: An example of ferry markings – two ex-US Navy R4Ds N10CA and N11CA from Naples are seen at Luton in August 1970.

Below: A number of DC-3s were used by oil companies in support of their North African operations; N487F of LAVCO is typical.

Left: Smart Mexican Air Force C-47 AP-0201 'Revolucionario' seen at Love Field, Dallas, on 2 October 1964.

Right: Dakota 4 KJ839 was used as a test-bed for Armstrong-Siddeley Mamba turboprops between 1949 and 1958, when it was restored to standard configuration.

Below left: Crop dusting with an unidentified DC-3; a large belly tank feeds the full-span spray bars.

Below: This US Navy R4D-5L 12418 became, on 31 October 1956, the first aircraft to land at the South Pole. It is preserved in the National Air and Space Museum, Washington, along with Eastern Air Lines DC-3 N18124. Note the skis plus JATO bottles beneath the fuselage.

Royal Aircraft Establishment's *Portpatrick Princess*, pictured in 1979.

Above: Silver City Airways bought C-53D G-AOBN and used it in the 1970s on radio calibration work before its sale to Egypt in 1977. It is shown at Le Touquet.

Below: In mid-1984 the Dutch Dakota Association acquired this ex-Finnish Air Force C-47 and flew it back to Amsterdam in early post-war KLM colours. The registration is appropriate and two of the sponsors are obvious. It is planned to keep the C-47 airworthy.

Variations

A major redesign of the DC-3/C-47 airframe was considered in 1947 to meet proposed new Civil Air Regulations which threatened existing DC-3s and C-47s, and Douglas engineers elected to attempt a modernization of the DC-3 airframe. Two aircraft, a C-47DL and a DC-3, were bought by the company to form prototypes of the new DC-3S, or Super DC-3. A 3 ft 3 in (99 cm) plug was inserted in the fuselage forward of the main spar, the fuselage was strengthened, new vertical and horizontal tail surfaces of increased area were fitted and new wing outer panels were designed with square-cut tips, reducing the span to 90 ft (27 m) and the wing area from 986 sq ft to 969 sq ft (92 m² to 90 m²). The whole engine nacelle design was cleaned up and had undercarriage doors which completely covered the undercarriage.

The first aircraft flew on 23 June 1949, with 1,475 hp Wright Cyclone R-1820-C9HE engines and showed a considerable performance increase, with maximum speed increasing from 230 to 270 mph (370 to 435 km/h) and cruising from 207 to 251 mph (333 to 404 km/h). The second aircraft flew with 1,450 hp Pratt & Whitney R-2000-D7 engines and both aircraft completed their flight trials successfully. A US sales tour, however, proved that the larger airlines were looking for something bigger, while the smaller ones, already operating DC-3s, could not afford the expense involved in uprating. The Super DC-3's commercial service was limited to one company, Capital Airlines, which bought three Cyclone-engined versions while other operators discovered that their current airworthiness certificates could after all be met.

The USAF bought the first prototype as the YC-129 (later YC-47F) but did not order; it differed from later models in having twin main wheels and could be fitted with JATO units. The USAF transferred it to the US Navy as the R4D-8X in 1951 and the Navy were sufficiently interested to order 100 conversions from existing R4D-5s, -6s and -7s, to be powered by 1,475 hp Wright Cyclone R-1820-80 engines. Some of these were also to serve with the US Marine Corps in Korea as flare carriers.

With the introduction of the Rolls-Royce Dart turboprop engine and the forthcoming delivery of Dart-powered Vickers Viscounts to British European Airways in 1953, the airline decided to use two DC-3s fitted with Dart 505 engines for turboprop familiarization flying. The aircraft, taken from BEA's fleet, were converted by Field Aircraft Services Ltd at Tollerton and the first entered service on 15 August 1951, flying from Northolt to Hanover with 1½ tons (1.5 tonnes) of cargo – they were not certificated for passenger carrying. Compared with the Dakota 3 and 4, the Dart Dakota was some 7 mph (11 km/h) slower in maximum speed but 13 mph (21 km/h) faster in cruising; the ceiling went up from 21,900 ft to 26,000 ft (6,675 m to 7,925 m) but the range was virtually halved from 1,100 miles to 650 miles (1,770 km to 1,046 km). The two aircraft performed a useful role before eventual conversion back to standard.

These were not, however, the first turboprop conversions; Armstrong Siddeley contracted Scottish Aviation at Prestwick to convert an ex-RAF Dakota 4 to take A.S. Mambas and this flew at Bitteswell on 27 August 1949. It was to serve as a test-bed for various marks of Mamba engine before being restored to standard configuration and sold in 1958.

Rolls-Royce bought a similar Dakota for testing Dart engines and this made its first Dart-powered flight from Hucknall, Nottingham, on 15 March 1950, remaining in service for some years until the standard engines were refitted and it was sold to a civil company.

The next turboprop DC-3 conversion was an American one, from a 20-year old airframe which started life in 1942 as a C-53. The Conroy Aircraft Corporation of Santa Barbara, California, specialised in the conversion of piston-powered aircraft to turboprops and in the spring of 1969 flew the Conroy Turbo-Three powered by two Rolls-Royce Dart 510 engines taken from a Viscount. The aircraft flew to the Paris Air Show in May 1969 and subsequently completed a 28-

Captain Giles Kershaw with the Tri Turbo Three N23SA in its Arctic colours.

The sleek line of the prototype Super DC-3 N30000 are apparent in this view with doors covering the mainwheels and a semi-retractable tailwheel. The picture is dated 20 July 1949.

nation demonstration tour. Conroy claimed that conversions would take only 30 days at the company's plant, but kits would be available for installation elsewhere. It was proposed to certificate the Turbo Three at 32,000 lb (14,515 kg) maximum take-off weight and a maximum cruise of 215 mph (346 km/h) at max AUW was claimed, plus a standard fuel range of 940 miles (1,513 km). The Darts were certificated at 1,600 shp but could be torque limited to 1,350 shp to match DC-3 certification and performance limits.

While the concept was interesting, there was no further development at that time but the same airframe turned up again in 1977 in a new guise as the Tri Turbo-Three built by the Tri Turbo Corporation for the Specialized Aircraft Company; Jack Conroy was President of the new company. Powered by three 1,174 eshp Pratt & Whitney PT6A-45A turboprops driving Hartzell five-blade propellers, the aircraft made its first flight, again at Santa Barbara, on 2 November 1977.

A cruising speed of 225 mph

(362 km/h) was claimed with the three turboprops providing 50 per cent more power than the two piston engines. Cost of a conversion kit at that time was quoted as $525,000 and around 3,000 man-hours of labour would be needed. Optional outboard wing tanks gave a range of more than 3,000 miles (4,828 km) and the aircraft could climb to 10,000 ft (3,048 m), shut down the centre engine and fly a 3,000 mile (4,828 km) mission with an hour's fuel reserve. The twin-engine cruising speed was 180 mph (290 km/h) and fuel consumption 108 US gallons (409 litres) per hour. The weight reduction of 2,500 lb (1,134 kg) from the basic DC-3 was said to give STOL characteristics, with reverse-pitch propellers giving a short landing run. Maintenance costs compared with the piston engine aircraft were considerably reduced; Conroy claimed that around 90 per cent of maintenance costs and man-hours on a standard DC-3 were spent on powerplant maintenance and on the Tri Turbo-Three this would be reduced to an average of 15 man-minutes per flight hour.

The aircraft appeared at the 1978 Farnborough Air Show – the first-ever DC-3 to do so – and attracted considerable attention. Demonstrations were made to a number of potential customers but failure to achieve FAA certification restricted the conversion to only the prototype aircraft. It was still around in the early 1980s, however, and was operated by Polair in support of a programme installing automatic hydrophones and electronic devices beneath the ice to measure the movement of marine life. One of the pilots, Captain Giles Kershaw, on leave from Britannia Airways, reported that the aircraft was 'a delight to

The sole USAF Super Dakota, originally designated YC-129 and later YC-47F, uses a battery of eight JATO bottles in a spectacular take-off. It was the only Super Dakota to have   mainwheels.

fly, but the exhaust stacks were in line with the cockpit window so that while taxiing for take-off one was blinded by watering eyes and virtually asphyxiated by the exhaust fumes; take-off brought little relief as the vibration and noise produced by the close proximity of the nose engine seemed to loosen all the bones in the body.' The cold caused innumerable problems with the engines and Captain Kershaw noted in his diary that over half his flying had been with at least one failed engine!

The most recent turbine-powered DC-3, the Turbo Express, has been produced by the United States Aircraft Corporation of Van Nuys, California. It comes as no surprise to see the name of Robert W. Lillibridge given as Vice-President of USAC; he had previously been V-P Engineering and Manufacturing with the Conroy Aircraft Corporation. USAC converted a DC-3 to take two 1,254 ehp Pratt & Whitney PT6A-45R turboprops with

Hartzell five-blade propellers and to counteract the 3,500 lb (1,588 kg) difference between the turboprop and piston engines a 3 ft 4 in (1 m) extension was added to the fuselage forward of the wing providing a useful increase in cabin volume. A number of other airframe modifications were incorporated, but externally the only one visible was a modified square-tipped tailplane. Extra tanks in the outer wing panels increased fuel capacity by 800 US gallons (3,028 l). Fuel consumption is an improvement on the Turbo Three at 100 US gallons (378 l) per hour at 190 mph (306 km/h) at 10,000 ft (3,048 m) and stalling speed is 64 mph (103 km/h).

First flight of the USAC Turbo Express was made on 28 July 1982 and a year later the company received an order for the first production conversion, a mixed configuration aircraft with capacity for 18 passengers in the front cabin and cargo at the rear. Details of further development are not known but Basler Airlines of

G-AMDB illustrates the experimental version with Rolls-Royce Dart turboprops.

Oshkosh, Wisconsin, have been named as a possible customer.

In the mid-1950s SFERMA in France fitted several types of aircraft with small underwing jet engines to improve take-off performance. Included in the programme was at least one French Air Force C-47 which had a 362 lb (164 kg) Turbomeca Palas turbojet beneath each wing.

An ex-RCAF Dakota, TS423, was used by the Ferranti Flying Unit for more than 14 years on trials with various forms of radar including the AI23 and 23B for the Lightning, Blue Parrot for the Buccaneer and forward looking radar for the TSR.2. The nose shape was modified a number of times to accommodate different radar fits. The Luftwaffe and other air forces similarly used Dakotas to test nose-mounted North American Search and Range Radar (NASARR) prior to installation in their F-104 Starfighters.

Specifications

Technical Description

Type: twin-engine military transport.
Wings: low-wing monoplane of all-metal cantilever construction. Rectangular centre-section and tapering outer sections with straight trailing edge and detachable wing-tips. Douglas cellular multo-web construction. Ailerons fabric covered, starboard aileron with controllable trim-tabs. All-metal hydraulically-operated split trailing-edge flaps. Rubber de-icer shoes on outer panel leading edges.
Fuselage: Almost circular-section with tranverse frames of formed sheet with a smooth sheet covering. Military versions (C-47 etc.) had provision for six parachute pack containers under fuselage plus glider towing equipment, a strengthened cargo floor with tie-down fittings and double cargo door in port side of fuselage; civil pre-war DC-3s had single passenger door in starboard side of fuselage.
Tail unit: cantilever fuselage-mounted tailplane. Tailplane and fin of multi-cellular metal construction, rudder and elevators with aluminium alloy frames and fabric covering, aerodynamically and statically balanced. All control surfaces with trim tabs. Rubber de-icer shoes on fin and tailplane leading edges.
Undercarriage: main wheels retracted forwards into engine nacelles leaving half-wheel exposed, and could be raised or lowered hydraulically in 15 seconds. Hydraulic wheel brakes, non-retractable steerable tail wheel.
Power plant and fuel system: engines mounted on bulkheads at front of centre section, each driving three-blade Hamilton Standard constant-speed propellers with de-icing. Two main fuel tanks each holding 202 US gallons (909 litres) forward of main spar in centre section with two 200 US gallons (900 litres) tanks behind the spar. Each engine had separate fuel system but crossfeed enabled engines to be fed from either tank. One 29 US gallons (130.5 litres) oil tank in each engine nacelle.
Accommodation: (DC-3) standard original layout for 28 passengers in the completely insulated cabin. Four mail cargo compartments forward of main cabin, two each side of centre aisle. Outside cargo loading door on port side behind pilot's seat. Baggage compartment at rear of cabin aft of buffet and toilet compartment. (C-47 etc) Crew of three, pilot, co-pilot and radio operator. Main cabin/cargo hold could accommodate up to 6,000 lb (2,725 kg) cargo (officially!) and folding seats down sides of cabin could take 28 equipped troops or parachutists. Fittings for 18 stretchers and accompanying three medical crew could be provided.

C-47 Variants

AC-47D	MATS Air Communications Service; 26 for airways checks
AC-47D	Designation used again in 1965 for Gunship modification
C-47H	1962 redesignation of USN R4D-5
C-47J	1962 redesignation of USN R4D-6
C-47M	Electronic reconnaissance conversion of C-47H and C-47J
EC-47D	1962 redesignation of first AC-47Ds
EC-47H	1962 redesignation of USN R4D-5Q
EC-47J	1962 redesignation of USN R4D-6Q
EC-47N	Electronic reconnaissance conversion of C-47As
EC-47P	Electronic reconnaissance conversion of C-47Ds
EC-47Q	Electronic reconnaissance conversion with R-2000-4 engines
HC-47D	1962 redesignation of SC-47A
LC-47H	1962 redesignation of USN R4D-5L
LC-47J	1962 redesignation of USN R4D-6L
RC-47A	Reconnaissance conversion of C-47A, used in Korea
RC-47D	Reconnaissance conversion of C-47D
SC-47A	Search and rescue conversion of C-47A
SC-47D	Search and rescue conversion of C-47D
SC-47H	1962 redesignation of USN R4D-5S
SC-47J	1962 redesignation of USN R4D-6S
TC-47B	Navigation trainer
TC-47D	Trainer conversion of C-47D
TC-47H	1962 redesignation of USN R4D-5R
TC-47J	1962 redesignation of USN R4D-6R
TC-47K	1962 redesignation of USN R4D-7
VC-47	Staff transport conversion of C-47
VC-47A	Staff transport conversion of C-47A
VC-47B	Staff transport conversion of C-47B
VC-47D	Staff transport conversion of C-47D
VC-47H	1962 redesignation of USN R4D-5Z
VC-47J	1962 redesignation of USN R4D-6Z
LC-117D	1962 redesignation of USN R4D-8L

R4D Variants

R4D-1	Cargo transport
R4D-2F	Two VIP aircraft, ex airline DC-3s. Redesignated R4D-2Z
R4D-2Z	See above
R4D-4Q	Radar countermeasures
R4D-4R	Ten airline DC-3s, impressed on production line
R4D-5E	Electronic equipment
R4D-5L	Arctic and Antarctic operations (1962 redesignated LC-47H)
R4D-5Q	Radar countermeasures (1962 redesignated EC-47H)
R4D-5R	Cargo aircraft converted to passenger transport (1962 redesignated TC-47H)
R4D-5S	Air-sea warfare trainer (1962 redesignated SC-47H)
R4D-5T	Navigation trainer
R4D-5Z	VIP interior (1962 redesignated VC-47H)
R4D-6E	Electronic equipment
R4D-6L	Arctic and Antarctic operations (1962 redesignated LC-47J)
R4D-6Q	Radar countermeasure (1962 redesignated EC-47J)
R4D-6R	Cargo aircraft converted to passenger transport (1962 redesignated TC-47J)
R4D-6S	Air-sea warfare trainer (1962 redesignated SC-47J)
R4D-6T	Navigation trainer
R4D-6Z	VIP interior (1962 redesignated VC-47J)
R4D-7	Navigation trainer (1962 redesignated TC-47K)
R4D-8	Super DC-3 evaluation prototype; 98 ordered, all conversions. (1962 redesignated C-117D)
R4D-8L	Winterized version for use in Antarctic (1962 redesignated LC-117D)
R4D-8T	Trainers (1962 redesignated TC-117D)
R4D-8X	Prototype R4D-8 transferred from USAF
R4D-8Z	Staff transports (1962 redesignated VC-117D)

Military DC-3 Variants

Designation/Number built

Designation	Number built	Description
C-41A	1	Command transport
C-47DL	965	First militarized DC-3 version for USAAF
C-47A-DL	2,954	24-volt system, improved heating
C-47A-DK	2,299	24-volt system, improved heating
C-47B-DL	300	High altitude version
C-47B-DK	2,932	High altitude version
TC-47B-DK	133	Navigational trainer
C-47C-DL	–	Amphibian conversion from C-47DL
C-47D	–	Conversions from C-47B
C-47E	–	Modified C-47 for airways checks
YC-47F	–	C-47DL conversion to Super DC-3, originally YC-129
C-48DO	1	Impressed on production line
C-48A-DO	3	Impressed on production line
C-48B-DO	16	Impressed from airlines
C-48C-DO	16	Impressed on production line (7); from airlines (9)
C-49DO	6	Impressed on production line
C-49A-DO	1	Impressed on production line
C-49B-DO	3	Impressed on production line
C-49C-DO	2	Impressed on production line
C-49D-DO	11	Impressed on production line (6); from airlines (5)
C-49E-DO	22	Impressed from airlines
C-49F-DO	9	Impressed from airlines
C-49G-DO	8	Impressed from airlines
C-49H-DO	19	Impressed from airlines
C-49J-DO	34	Impressed on production line
C-49K-DO	23	Impressed on production line
C-50DO	4	Impressed on production line
C-50A-DO	2	Impressed on production line
C-50B-DO	3	Impressed on production line
C-50C-DO	1	Impressed on production line
C-50D-DO	4	Impressed on production line
C-51DO	1	Impressed on production line
C-52DO	1	Impressed on production line
C-52A-DO	1	Impressed on production line
C-52B-DO	2	Impressed on production line
C-52C-DO	1	Impressed on production line
C-52D-DO	1	Impressed from airline
C-53DO	221	Skytrooper troop transport
C-53C-DO	17	Impressed on production line
C-53D-DO	159	Skytrooper, sideways facing seats
C-68DO	2	Impressed on production line
C-84DO	4	Impressed from airlines
C-84DO	12	Impressed on production line, undesignated
C-117A-DK	17	Staff transport
C-117B-DK	–	Conversions from C-117A, blowers removed
C-117C	–	Overhauled C-47s upgraded to C-117B standard
C-117D	–	Redesignation of R4D-8 Super DC-3
XCG-17	–	Glider conversion from C-47DL
R4D-1	66	USN aircraft, C-47DL standard, 40 more ex USAAF
R4D-2	2	USN, impressed on production line
R4D-3	–	USN, 20 personnel transports, ex USAAF C-53DO
R4D-4	10	USN, impressed on production line
R4D-5	–	USN, 81 C-47A-DL and 157 C-47A-DK from USAAF
R4D-6	–	USN, 150 C-47B-DK from USAAF
R4D-7	–	USN, 41 TC-47B-DK trainers from USAAF

Military production and impressment	10,289
Pre-war civil	430
Post-war civil	28
	10,747
Less civil impressments	93
Total production:	10,654

Douglas DC-1

Type: Commercial transport
Accommodation: crew of two and 12 passengers
Powerplant: two 710 hp (529 kW) Wright Cyclone SGR-1820-F3 nine-cylinder radial engines
Performance:
maximum speed 210 mph (388 km/h) at 8,000 ft (2,438 m)
cruising speed 200 mph (322 km/h) at 14,000 ft (4,268 m)
climb rate 1,050 ft/min (320 m/min)
service ceiling 23,000 ft (7,010 m)
range 1,000 miles (1,609 km)
Weights:
empty 11,780 lb (5,343 kg)
loaded 17,500 lb (7,938 kg)
Dimensions:
span 85 ft 0 in (25.91 m)
length 60 ft 0 in (18.29 m)
height 16 ft 0 in (4.88 m)
wing area 942 sq ft (87.515 m²)

Douglas C-39

Type: Military transport
Accommodation: crew of three and 12 passengers or 3,600 lb (1,633 kg) of cargo
Powerplant: two 975 hp (727 kW) Wright Cyclone R-1820-55 nine-cylinder radial engines
Performance:
maximum speed 210 mph (338 km/h) at 5,000 ft (1,524 m)
cruising speed 156 mph (251 km/h) at 5,000 ft (1,524 m)
climb rate 1,480 ft/min (451 m/min)
service ceiling 20,600 ft (6,280 m)
range 1,600 miles (2,575 km)
Weights:
empty 14,287 lb (6,481 kg)
loaded 21,000 lb (9,526 kg)
max. loaded 26,300 lb (11,929 kg)
Dimensions:
span 85 ft 0 in (25.91 m)
length 61 ft 10 in (18.85 m)
height 18 ft 8 in (5.69 m)
wing area 939 sq ft (87.24 m²)

Douglas DST

Type: Commercial sleeper transport
Accommodation: crew of two plus stewardess; 14 passengers in sleeping berths or 28 in day seating
Powerplant: two 850 hp (634 kW) Wright Cyclone SGR-1820-G2 nine-cylinder radial engines
Performance:
maximum speed 212 mph (341 km/h) at 6,800 ft (2,075 m)
cruising speed 192 mph (309 km/h)
climb rate 850 ft/min (259 m/min)
service ceiling 20,800 ft (6,340 m)
range 1,250 miles (2,010 km)
Weights:
empty 16,060 lb (7,285 kg)
loaded 24,000 lb (10,886 kg)
Dimensions:
span 95 ft 0 in (28.96 m)
length 64 ft 5½ in (19.65 m)
height 16 ft 3¾ in (4.97 m)
wing area 987 sq ft (91.7 m²)

Douglas C-47B

Type: Military transport
Accommodation: crew of three, up to 6,000 lb (2,725 kg) of cargo or 28 parachute troops in folding seats or 14 stretchers and three attendants
Powerplant: two 1,000 hp (746 kW) Pratt & Whitney R-1830-90C 14-cylinder radial engines
Performance:
maximum speed 224 mph (360 km/h) at 10,000 ft (3,050 m)
cruising speed 160 mph (257 km/h)
climb rate 9.5 minutes to 10,000 ft (3,050 m)
service ceiling 26,400 ft (8,045 m)
range 1,600 miles (2,575 km)
Weights:
empty 18,135 lb (8,226 kg)
loaded 26,000 lb (11,793 kg)
max. loaded 31,000 lb (14,061 kg)
Dimensions:
span 95 ft 6 in (29.11 m)
length 63 ft 9 in (19.43 m)
height 17 ft 0 in (5.18 m)
wing area 987 sq ft (91.7 m^2)

Showa L2D3-1a

Type: Military transport
Accommodation: crew of three to five and 21 passengers or 9,920 lb (4,500 kg) of freight
Powerplant: two 1,300p (969 kW) Mitsubishi Kinsei 53 14-cylinder radial engines
Performance:
maximum speed 244 mph (393 km/h) at 9,185 ft (2,800 m)
cruising speed 150 mph (241 km/h) at 9,845 ft (3,000 m)
climb rate 16 minutes to 16,400 ft (5,000 m)
service ceiling –
range 1,864 miles (3,000 km)
Weights:
empty 15,913 lb (7,218 kg)
loaded 27,558 lb (12,500 kg)
Dimensions:
span 95 ft 0 in (28.96 m)
length 64 ft 0 in (19.5 m)
height 24 ft 5¾ in (7.46 m)
wing area 985.9 sq ft (91.6 m^2)

Lisunov Li-2

Type: Military transport
Accommodation: probably similar to C-47
Powerplant: two 900 hp (671 kW) Shvetsov M-62 nine-cylinder radial engines
Performance:
maximum speed 174 mph (280 km/h)
cruising speed 137 mph (220 km/h)
climb rate –
service ceiling 18,375 ft (5,600 m)
range –
Weights:
empty 16,976 lb (7,700 kg)
loaded 23,589 lb (10,700 kg)
max. loaded 24,868 lb (11,280 kg)
Dimensions:
span 94 ft 10¼ in (28.81 m)
length 64 ft 5¾ in (19.65 m)
height 16 ft 11 in (5.2 m)
wing area 983 sq ft (91.33 m^2)

Douglas DC-3C

Type: Commercial transport
Accommodation: crew of two plus stewardess; 28 passengers
Powerplant: two 1,050 hp (783 kW) Pratt & Whitney Twin Wasp R-1830-92 14-cylinder radial engines
Performance:
maximum speed 237 mph (381 km/h) at 8,000 ft (2,680 m)
cruising speed 170 mph (274 km/h)
climb rate 1,130 ft/min (344 m/min)
service ceiling 23,200 ft (7,071 m)
range 1,025 miles (1,650 km)
Weights:
empty 18,300 lb (8,301 kg)
loaded 25,200 lb (11,431 kg)
max. loaded 28,000 lb (12,701 kg)
Dimensions:
span 95 ft 0 in (28.96 m)
length 64 ft 5 in (19.63 m)
height 16 ft 11 in (5.16 m)
wing area 987 sq ft (91.7 m^2)

Douglas R4D-8

Type: Military transport
Accommodation: crew of three and 33 passengers or 27 stretchers
Powerplant: two 1,475 hp (1,100 kW) Wright Cyclone R-1820-80 14-cylinder radial engines
Performance:
maximum speed 270 mph (432 km/h) at 5,900 ft (1,800 m)
cruising speed 251 mph (401 km/h)
climb rate 1,300 ft/min (396 m/min)
service ceiling –
range 2,500 miles (4,025 km)
Weights:
empty 19,537 lb (8,870 kg)
loaded 31,000 lb (14,075 kg)
Dimensions:
span 90 ft 0 in (27.43 m)
length 67 ft 9 in (20.75 m)
height 18 ft 3 in (5.56 m)
wing area 969 sq ft (90.023 m^2)

Tri Turbo Corporation Tri Turbo-Three

Type: Cargo transport
Accommodation: payload 9,140 lb (4,145 kg) with 800 US gallons of fuel
Powerplant: three 1,174 ehp (875.5 kW) Pratt & Whitney of Canada PT6A-45 turboprops
Performance:
maximum speed –
cruising speed 220 mph (354 km/h) at 5,000 ft (1,524 m)
climb rate –
service ceiling –
range 1,135 miles (1,826 km)
Weights:
empty 14,000 lb (6,350 kg)
max. loaded 29,000 lb (13,150 kg)
Dimensions:
span 94 ft 0 in (28.65 m)
length 72 ft 0 in (21.94 m)
height 17 ft 0 in (5.18 m)
wing area 987 sq ft (91.7 m^2)

Acknowledgements

I am most grateful to friends and fellow enthusiasts for help received in collecting photographs for this Profile. In particular Harry Gann, Geoff Norris and Karen Stubberfield of McDonnell Douglas supplied many interesting photos (as may be seen by the credits!); Malcolm Smith of Fokker provided rare pre-war pictures while other suppliers included Jack Titley of Rolls-Royce, John Elliott of Swissair, Jan Willem de Wijn of the Schiphol Airport Authority and the Dutch Dakota Association, Han Kock of KLM, Ken Meadows of the Royal Aircraft Establishment, Farnborough, Charles W. Cain, John Stroud and Barry Wheeler. My thanks also to a number of unidentified photographers whose pictures I used but could not acknowledge.

Last but by no means least, like most writers who spend all their time researching and scribbling, my thanks to my wife Pam for transferring my notes to the typewriter, thus easing the typesetter's task!

Credits

All pictures supplied by Mike J. Hooks, except for the following:
Aerophoto-Schiphol BV: p. 49.
Air-Britain: p. 43 (bottom).
British Airways: p. 53, endpapers.
Erwin J. Bulban: pp. 37 & 44 (top).
Ferranti Ltd.: p. 35 (bottom).
Flight: p. 28.
Fokker: p. 5 (top), p. 8 (both).
Handley Page Ltd.: p. 29 (bottom).
K. Hyde: p. 43 (centre).

Giles Kershaw: p. 48.
KLM: pp. 14 (right), 40/41, 42 (top).
McDonnell Douglas Corp.: pp. 9 (both), 10, 12, 13, 14 *(Left)*, 15, 16, 25, 26, 27, 29 (top), 34, 35 (top), 36, 38 (bottom), 44 (bottom), 45 (bottom), 48, 50/51, 52.
A. Le Nobel: p. 43 (top).
RAE Farnborough: pp. 46/47.
Rolls-Royce Ltd.: p. 45 (top).
Jerry Scutts: p. 39.
John Stroud: pp. 30/31, 32.
Swissair Photo AG: p. 4 (bottom).
Simon R.P. Thomson: p. 35 (centre).

Colour section: All pictures by M.J. Hooks, except the following:
Jerry Scutts (USAF): p. 17 (top).
McDonnell Douglas: p. 17 (bottom).
Stuart Howe: pp. 22 and 23.
Candid Aero-Files: p. 24 (both).